MW00414385

Daniel Nash

Laborer with Finney. Mighty in Prayer

Steve Porter

Daniel Nash

Laborer with Finney. Mighty in Prayer

Copyright © 2021 Steve Porter

All rights reserved.

All Artwork Copy written © by Deeper Life Press

ISBN: 978-1-64713-828-8

Deeper Life Press

Dedication

To my beautiful daughter Alyssa and my Son-in-law Ethan

For what you both carry the next generation so desperately needs.

May the Lord use you both to light a fresh fire in the next Great Awakening!

"Confess your faults one to another, and pray one for another, that ye may be healed. The effectual fervent prayer of a righteous man availeth much."
(James 5:16)

"Hear the supplications of your servant and of your people Israel when they pray toward this place. Hear from heaven, your dwelling place; and when you hear, forgive."
(2 Chronicles 6:21)

"Said Father Nash was a most wonderful man in prayer, one of the most earnest, devout, spiritually-minded, heavenly-minded men I ever saw. . . . He labored about in many places in central and northern New York, and gave himself up to almost constant prayer, literally praying himself to death at last. I have been informed that he was found dead in his room in the attitude of prayer."
— Charles Finney on Daniel Nash, his chief intercessor.

Acknowledgments

Special thanks to our editors Nancy Arant Williams, Emer Garry, Ken Darrow and our Deeper Life Press publishing team.

Deepest gratitude to my good friend Sue Kopczyk for the sketch idea we used to create the men praying cover art.

Special thanks also to our Refuge Ministries Partners for your prayers, generous support, and kind encouragement that helped this book find a voice.

Most of all, our eternal gratitude goes to our Beloved Father, who holds us so close in the palm of His hand.

Table of Contents

Preface

DANIEL
NASH
LABORER WITH
FINNEY
MIGHTY IN PRAYER
Nov. 17, 1775
Dec. 20, 1831

The short book you now hold in your hands is the story of an incredibly anointed man by the name of Daniel Nash. It was difficult for me to find factual information on Daniel Nash as there are only two books written on the life of this great prayer warrior, one of which is now out of print. His prayer story has impacted my life like no other, and it wasn't long before I realized that the Lord was calling me to bring his story to life in a fresh, accurate way. I have spent the last few years studying the life of Charles Finney and unearthed everything I could find on Nash's life. To further enhance Father Nash's story, I have included helpful history about the effects of the Second Great Awakening and how God used the fervent prayers of Daniel Nash and Abel Clary to impact Charles Finney's far-reaching evangelistic efforts. I also draw many prophetic applications from his life and experiences that I hope will encourage you. My prayer is that this book will inspire other forerunners of revival to use their own fervent prayers to exponentially impact the world with the Gospel. That intercession would again open the way for another powerful awakening that this world has yet to see.

There are no known pictures of the Presbyterian Nash. Please note the artwork I had commissioned for this very book is actually the image of another Father Nash altogether. I explain more about this within the book. I did this for two reasons. **1. There are no known images of the Presbyterian Father Nash and 2. So many now affiliate him with the Christ Church portrait and I am using that image as a point of reference only.**

For as the waters fill the sea, the earth will be filled with an awareness of the glory of the LORD (Hab. 2:14).

Prayerfully,
Steve Porter

Introduction

O nce, not long ago, on a dark, rainy day, I made my way over wet ground to a very special place. A chill trembled through me as the cold rain pelted my skin, drenching me to the bone. Still I walked, eager to get to my destination—the very place where Father Daniel Nash's church once stood, though his name may be unfamiliar to most. He was born in 1775 and, at age forty, began to minister for six years as a preacher in Upstate New York, where he saw two great revivals during a short period of time. It's said that he didn't trust in his own spoken words or cleverly written sermons to change the hearts of his listeners but knew that only prevailing prayer could summon the presence of the Holy Spirit to transform the culture of the day.

Unfortunately, at age forty-three, he was voted out of his church—by a vote of nine to three—because they were annoyed by his frequent travels to preach, and they let him go in favor of a younger man. With a humble heart he continued to serve the people there, filling the pulpit when needed and seeing many people saved because of his fervent prayers. He struggled with the pain of rejection and felt he would be of little use to the Kingdom of God, but God had a greater plan!

A few years later, God laid the need for a forerunner on his heart to intercede before and during the revival meetings held by Evangelist Charles Finney. In fact, he made a habit of going several days before the beginning of a revival, locating an out-of-the-way, tiny, dark, often damp space to rent, then finding two or three like-minded individuals to fast and pray with him, groaning in the spirit for hours and days at a time. It's said that a holy light filled the dim room, making it a powerful place to intercede and believe God would move as never before.

A monument of his image and name stands on the front step (where this foundation rock of the steps still sits) where his church once stood, and today that parcel of land, owned by Dwelling Place Ministries of Lowville, NY, has been set aside with great expectations for a future powerful revival move of God. (In fact, on that rainy day I mentioned above, I had a wonderful time ministering in that amazing church.)

Afterward, we drove a few miles to visit a neglected cemetery called **Stowe Square Cemetery**, tucked away in the same village, in Lewis County, New York, not far from the Canadian border. As I visited the gravesite of Father Nash, I stood fighting the wind and rain with my umbrella but felt a powerful presence as I read the faded wording on his tombstone:

DANIEL NASH
Laborer with Finney
Mighty in Prayer
Nov. 17, 1775 – Dec. 20, 1831

"Mighty in Prayer." What an epitaph to sum up a life! It was said that Daniel Nash was mighty in prayer and he truly was, so much so that we might even dare to emulate such things in our day. Will we pay such a price for revival?

My weekend was filled with meetings and a strong manifestation of His presence. I was honored to visit that place and felt I was there by divine appointment. It was as if God had something to share with me, especially when He said, **"Like the rain you now feel upon your skin so Daniel Nash was wet with tears from deep groaning and intercession."** It's been said that Daniel Nash prayed so hard that his nose began to bleed, and he would be wet with perspiration even during the dark, cold New York winters. He was physically exhausted when he finally went to bed. As he fervently prayed, he shook the very heavens above him. Let me introduce you to Father Nash, a man after God's own heart.

Chapter 1

Daniel Nash: "MIGHTY IN PRAYER"

"There can be no revival when Mr. Amen and Mr. Wet-Eyes are not found in the audience."
– Charles Finney

This is the story of a modest man whose fervent prayers inspired a revival like none other. He lived during the time Charles Finney was traveling wherever the Spirit moved him to preach the Gospel of Salvation. It was then that the Holy Spirit spoke to the heart of an unknown man by the name of Daniel Nash, urging him to pray for the power to encounter Finney's evangelistic services.

As a result of his powerful prayers, Heaven opened and crowds rushed to the revival altars, so that even the hardest of hearts supernaturally turned toward the Lord, never to be the same again. In fact, Nash's prayers were so effective that Finney's services reverted to ordinariness after Nash died and was no longer praying, but let's not get ahead of ourselves here.

Not many people recognized his name during his time, while others paid little attention to him, but God knew his name. Daniel Nash was a man of God and a man of rare humility. The devil also knew his name and trembled every time he entered the room. His prayers carried a mighty power and authority while aflame with a burning love for Christ.

Though his birthplace is unknown, we know he was born in the US in 1775. While little is known about his early life, it's recorded that he was called to pastor in a Presbyterian church, where seventy people were saved in a small revival during his first year there.

Daniel Nash began his ministry in Upstate New York. He saw revival twice in his pastorate and was a key figure in one of the greatest revivals in US history.

Someone once asked Finney what kind of man Father Nash was, and why they never see him enter any of the meetings. Finney replied, **"like anybody who does a lot of praying, Father Nash is a very quiet person. Show me a person who is always talking, and I'll show you a Christian who never does much praying."**

Fervency in Prayer

The Word of God gives us many shining examples of those who prayed with all their hearts, souls and minds in both the Old and New Testaments. We can see it throughout church history as well.

These people seen genuine conversions as many repented and received Christ in numbers that were off the charts, but, even more importantly, changed their lives forever.

Unfortunately, things are much different today, as perhaps only 20% of evangelistic attendees are saved, and only half that number stay the course for a lifetime. When was the last time you saw someone collapse in fervent prayer?

In the words of Charles Finney on Nash's last moments on Earth: "Said a good man to me: 'Oh, I am dying for the want of strength to pray! My body is crushed, the world is on me, and how can I forbear praying?' I have known that man go to bed absolutely sick, for weakness and faintness, under the pressure. And I have known him pray as if he would do violence to Heaven, and then have seen the blessing come as plainly in answer to his prayer as if it were revealed, so that no person could doubt it any more than if God had spoken from Heaven. Shall I tell you how he died? He prayed more and more; he used to take the map of the world before him, and pray, and look over the different countries and pray for them, till he expired in his room, praying. Blessed man! He was the reproach of the ungodly, and of carnal, unbelieving professors; but he was the favorite of Heaven, and a prevailing prince of prayer."

These are fervent prayers for intercession, but the cost to our physical bodies of that kind of prayer needs to be mentioned. From Finney notes:

"I have never known a person sweat blood, but I have known a person pray till the blood started from his nose. And I have known persons pray till they were all wet with perspiration in the coldest weather in winter. I have known persons pray for hours till their strength was all exhausted with the agony of their minds..."

That kind of prayer staggers my imagination, yet it is amply recorded for us to see and hopefully give us a testimony to follow and learn from. Crying out to God, weeping, with not enough strength left to even stand up is powerful prayer that goes so deep and is so gut-wrenching that it literally robs the limbs of strength. How could that happen?

Intercession on behalf of other sinners that weighed heavily on these men who so loved those very same lost souls meant they risked their health to stir the power of the Holy Spirit.

Matthew 22:3 tells us, "The second most important commandment is like this one. And it is "**Love others as much as you love yourself**." (Emphasis mine)

To sow into the spirit through deep intercession brings tremendous lessons. We can learn from men like these, both from a personal perspective and when we take on the responsibility of praying for others. To love others as much as we do our own lives and families is a rare thing indeed.

In light of the life and the sacrifices made by men like Daniel Nash, perhaps all of us will think twice before we throw out the phrase, "I'll pray for you." Though few of us carry the same passionate burden, zeal and motivation as Daniel Nash, God is raising up forerunners and prototypes for this kind of ministry in these end times.

Philippians 4:9 The things you have learned and received and heard and seen in me, practice these things, and the God of peace will be with you (NASB: Lockman)

Greek: a kai emathete (2PAAI) kai parelabete (2PAAI) kai ekousate (2PAAI) kai eidete (2PAAI) en emoi, tauta **prassete; (2PPAM**) kai o theos tes eirenes estai (3SPAI) meth' humon

Amplified: Practice what you have learned and received and heard and seen in me, and model your way of living on it, and the God of peace (of untroubled, undisturbed well-being) will be with you (Amplified Bible - Lockman)

NLT: Keep putting into practice all you learned from me and heard from me and saw me doing, and the God of peace will be with you. (NLT - Tyndale House)

Phillips: Model your conduct on what you have learned from me, on what I have told you and shown you, and you will find the God of peace will be with you (Phillips: Touchstone)

Wuest: The things also which you learned and received and heard and saw in me, these things habitually practice, and the God of peace shall be with you.

Young's Literal: the things that also ye did learn, and receive, and hear, and saw in me, those do, and the God of the peace shall be with you.

Brethren, join in following my example, and observe those who walk according to the pattern you have in us. (Philippians 3:17)

In his letter to the Philippians, Apostle Paul instructed us to "Said a good man to me: 'Oh, I am dying for the want of strength to pray! My body is crushed, the world is on me, and how can I forbear praying?' I have known that man go to bed absolutely sick, for weakness and faintness, under the pressure. And I have known him pray as if he would do violence to Heaven, and then have seen the blessing come as plainly in answer to his prayer as if it were revealed, so that no person could doubt it any more than if God had spoken from Heaven. Shall I tell you how he died? He prayed more and more; he used to take the map of the world before him, and pray, and look over the different countries and pray for them, till he expired in his room, praying. Blessed man! He was the reproach of the ungodly, and of carnal, unbelieving professors; but he was the favorite of Heaven, and a prevailing prince of prayer." his example of imitating the great men and women who've preceded us. Some of the role models we should emulate include George Whitfield, who ministered for thirty-five years, preaching 30,000 sermons for more hours than he slept during any given week. He traversed the Atlantic Ocean thirteen times and experienced scorn, rejection, ridicule, and death threats and even found himself dodging hurled objects like dead cats, rocks and dung, and yet he stayed the course.

David Brainerd (1800s) may be an unfamiliar name because he never sought notoriety. In fact, he lived in isolation in the American wilderness, riding 15,000 miles on horseback to minister to the American Indians for whom he was deeply burdened, going days on end without food and eventually dying of tuberculosis at only 29.

What about Mary Slessor, a blue-eyed redhead from Scotland, who went to Nigeria to minister to the lost? Because the Efik people believed twins were a curse from the devil, she rescued hundreds of infant twins that were abandoned, left to die or to be eaten by wild animals. She traveled great distances, sharing the Gospel of Christ, while suffering from ongoing bouts of malaria, until it finally took her life at age 66. That's what a true calling looks like.

Then there's William Carey, an Englishman who traveled to India in 1793, where his wife soon went insane and died; then he endured the death of one of his infant sons soon afterward. During his first year there, he had to work as a menial laborer after the theft of all his funds in order to support his family. During his 41-year stay there, he translated scripture into over 25 Indian dialects, never once returning home. If that isn't sacrifice, what is?

John Paton left Scotland and sailed to the New Hebrides with his wife and infant son, who soon died from a tropical disease. Then he made his home with cannibals he called "beloved" who had previously killed and eaten any white man whose foot touched their island shores. How many of us would've dared to go so far as to live and die that way in service to God?

This chapter wouldn't be complete if we failed to mention Elisabeth Elliot, who moved with several other missionary families to South America to minister to the notorious Auca Indian tribe, who ultimately killed her husband and the missionaries who were with him. However, when the other missionary widows made arrangements to move home, she made plans to move with her young daughter into the Auca village to continue her husband's legacy, preaching and winning over lost souls.

The Apostle Paul himself penned eight chapters of foundational doctrine, only to say, "I am telling the truth in Christ, I am not lying, my conscience testifies with me in the Holy Spirit, that I have great sorrow and unceasing grief in my heart. For I could wish that I myself were accursed (the Greek word is anathema), separated from Christ for the sake of my brethren, my kinsman according to the flesh," (Rom. 9:1-3). He was saying that he would exchange his life and all that he had if only the Jews would turn to Christ and be saved. For that, he suffered condemnation, scourging, shipwrecks, and many other hardships and counted it all as nothing compared to the inestimable joy of winning souls for Christ. In the end Paul gave up his very life as a martyr for the Gospel's sake.

Just like Father Nash, each of these amazing people also gave their relentless passion and love for the sake of the Gospel. That kind of vision is rare, but God is searching high and low for those who will catch the vision and touch the world, no matter the cost, to win one. What about you? Will you answer the call?

Chapter 2

THE DARK NIGHT OF THE SOUL

"I was surprised to see him looking all over the house, as if he were talking to the people; while in fact he was praying to God. Of course, it did not sound to me much like prayer; and he was at that time indeed in a very cold and backslidden state." – *Charles Finney on Daniel Nash, his chief intercessor.*

Charles Finney was born in Warren, Connecticut in 1792. He was a truly incredible man, whom some have called an apostle of revival. He was one of the most powerful Spirit-filled evangelist ministers of his day, as well as the most widely-used evangelist in history, in both the US and Great Britain. In fact, everywhere he preached during his 40-year career, he was instrumental in kindling powerful revivals, bringing thousands of unbelievers to Christ. I have dedicated a whole chapter to the remarkable relationship between Finney and Father Nash, who joined hearts to pray and preach, turning the world on its ear.

While traveling in Upstate New York in the mid-1820s, Charles Finney met Daniel Nash, who at the time appeared broken and was in a spiritually cold, backslidden state. Perhaps it was due to the rejection he'd experienced at the hands of a congregation to whom he'd ministered for three years. It's true that he had often traveled to preach, but he sometimes returned home to take care of church business. It may also be that the combination of his advanced age and his frequent absences due to travel turned the people against him. Whatever the cause, he was a depressed and broken man. By 1824, he was so spiritually despondent that any hope of ministry seemed out of the question. At that time,

Finney himself was assigned to go before the board of examiners in order to obtain his license to preach. He described his initial meeting with Father Nash this way:

"At this meeting of the presbytery I first saw Rev. Daniel Nash, who is generally known as 'Father Nash.' He was a member of the presbytery. A large congregation was assembled to hear my examination. I got in a little late, and saw a man standing in the pulpit speaking to the people, as I supposed. He looked at me, I observed, as I came in; and was looking at others as they passed up the aisles. As soon as I reached my seat and listened, I observed that he was praying. I was surprised to see him looking all over the house, as if he were talking to the people; while in fact he was praying to God. Of course, it did not sound to me much like prayer; and he was at that time indeed in a very cold and backslidden state."

Shortly after their meeting, Father Nash was stricken with a serious eye inflammation, which was probably an infection as it was severe enough to dim his vision for several weeks. There was no effective treatment before the advent of antibiotics, and the conditions of that day left something to be desired, so he chose to stay in a dark room, to soothe them, though he could neither read nor write there. During this dark season of his soul, Father Nash gave himself completely over to ceaseless, fervent prayer, so that, in the end, his walk with God was totally transformed.

The Purpose of the Dark Night

As darkness seems to fall on us in different seasons of life, we can grow increasingly desperate to find our one true love, Jesus; though at times our search can appear to be in vain when we're blinded by confusion and pain and God seems farther away than ever.

At times we too may feel alone and anxious, abandoned and afraid, unable to sense His presence anywhere. In that regard, I can imagine Daniel Nash's face—his eyes hollow and haunted, feeling rejected and confused. He must have wondered how his beloved church could have betrayed him. Still, in the depths of his pain he cried out to Jesus, desperate for comfort, and ended up discovering His greatness at the very worst time of his life.

Can you imagine how shocked he was to experience the depth of God's great love while feeling more worthless than he'd ever felt in his life? So how did he respond? He ran into those loving arms and refused to let Him go! Over and over he poured out his heart and felt God pour oil onto his wounds, trading ashes for brand-new hope. In that moment, he also discovered his destiny and the reason why he was born: to pray fervently!

At some point, you may face a dark night when it seems that all is lost, so that your spiritual vision becomes blurred and you can no longer sense His nearness. The sense of abandonment can be palpable, and God feels a million miles away. Perhaps you're in that battle now. Well, hold on to hope because the truth is that He's only a prayer away.

When you reach out to those around you, they don't understand, nor can they help you. All at once you discover a deep desperation within that you didn't know existed. It propels you from that place of spiritual apathy into a full-blown pursuit of your Lord. Your spiritual hunger begins to grow by leaps and bounds inside you, so that nothing but His presence will suffice you.

It might help to know that there's a purpose to the dark night of the soul: our deep needs motivate us to earnestly seek our one true love. If we understood what was going on, we would actually short-circuit the process. It's the not knowing that creates a yearning for God, motivating us to rise up to pursue Him. We must permit it to run its course in order to accomplish God's objectives in our lives. I'm sure Father Nash felt exactly that way before he finally broke through the hazy fog.

Darkness always vanishes with the sunrise and with it comes hope for the new season you're facing. With this new day comes the revelation that even in your darkest moment, you were never alone. His presence was still there with you, yet it was hidden so that you would desire Him and pursue Him above all else. Can you truly say that you love Him more than anything or anyone else?

Clearly that was the case with Daniel Nash, who came to the end of himself and cried out to God in desperation, yearning for His presence.

Before apathy falls away, we experience severe heart-ache and pain, feeling as if we're out on a limb alone with nowhere to turn. At that point we cease to focus on ourselves, realizing that we won't make it unless God shows up in our circumstances because only His presence will suffice; nothing else can even come close. In fact, everything else fades away in the light of His presence during the dark night of the soul.

If you're in a dark season, it's time to rise up, my dear friend, and pursue the object of your affection! Wait on the Lord and refuse to succumb to your feelings. Just know that the morning is coming when you will soar as high as an eagle. You will run and not grow weary. You will walk and not faint!

The phrase "dark night of the soul" sounds like a threatening and much-to-be-avoided experience. Yet, if we never experienced the terrible loneliness of the frigid dark winter, it's unlikely that we would yearn for the warmth of the sun. In the dark night we learn to beseech God, with deep travail, before

He comes to make everything new inside us. It's in the dark night that we are healed of deep wounds and experience a holy desperation for our heavenly Father.

As we study the life of Daniel Nash, it's clear that this is exactly what happened to him. His physical eyes were affected so that he was in a literal dark room, but the despair of his soul brought on even greater darkness within. I believe it was during this discouraging season that God was preparing him to become the catalyst for a mighty revival.

Biblical history often demonstrates God's supernatural ability to use broken men and women. The truth is, unless we come to that place of brokenness, we remain essentially useless to the Kingdom of God because we're still too full of ourselves. No doubt those amazing Bible stories motivate us to seek God for ourselves, but we're even inspired when we hear stories of men in recent years that were used in such powerful ways. If He can use other desperate people, perhaps He can use us too.

Father Nash's **desperate heart cry** that originated from God birthed the ongoing travailing in prayer that brought thousands of lost souls to Christ. His wasn't a normal prayer in English because praying in English meant the mind was still in control of the process, while praying in the spirit actually touched the yearning of God's own heart and brought forth miraculous fruit in ways that would have otherwise been impossible.

We mustn't forget that Nash was a thoughtful, contemplative soul. He was not charismatic or gifted, but his humble yielded heart and his ceaseless prayers enabled Finney to greatly multiply his efforts in the Spirit.

In the end, Father Nash emerged from his dark night a healed and changed man—a powerhouse of influence that wreaked havoc on the kingdom of darkness. Not only was his physical eyesight restored, but his faith grew exponentially, so that he could believe in God. From that point on, he abandoned the idea of only preaching and personal evangelism, knowing that he was born to fervently pray.

From that humble beginning came the dawn of the 1820s 'Dream Team'. Daniel Nash, later accompanied by another deeply prayerful man named Abel

Clary, reconnected with Charles Finney, and the team went to work in the region of Evans Mills, New York. Finney described Nash this way: "He was full of the power of prayer."

It is here that I must pause and clear up a misunderstanding regarding Nash and Finney. It has been said that Nash had prayer meetings before every conference that Finney had. We know this is not true as a historical letter was found between Nash and Finney where Nash asked him why he did not bring him more often. You could sense a disappointment in Nash as you read the account. There is no proof that Nash was at every single meeting with Finney. We can prove he was at a few, but not all. However, with that said, I personally believe although Nash was not physically at all the meetings, he gave himself to fervent intercession behind the scenes from his home. This is my opinion as we know that Father Nash carried a burden for Charles Finney and revival and we plainly see the results of his prayer until Nash's homecoming to Heaven. Once Daniel Nash passed away so the revival and the ministry of Charles Finney dissipated.

A District Burned Over

It was the mid-1830s when the Second Great Awakening peaked, and many new churches opened across the country, especially in New England. It was accompanied by such an increased air of expectancy that the revivals in Upstate New York and Canada were called 'burned over districts.' In the same way that a forest fire can sweep away everything in front of it, the Holy Spirit began doing new work, shattering old religious views and changing everything in its wake. Instead of simply going through the motions of religion, people were spontaneously acting and speaking as the Holy Spirit moved them in the moment.

In some places, it wasn't an easy sell. In fact, Finney himself actually coined the term 'burnt district' in his book, *Autobiography of Charles G. Finney*, written in 1876. In it, he used the term to describe certain areas of New York State. It wasn't a compliment; it described people who had been wildly excited by the idea of a mighty move of God that, in reality, had never happened. Apparently, during that time, many other revivals had been going on in the area, but most were short-lived and had no lasting impact on the people there. Its impact on Finney was profound because when he scheduled true revival meetings in those areas, he found that they were rife with angry, bitter people who thought of religion as a fraudulent thing with no authenticity anywhere. In other words, they felt that all religion was nothing but smoke and mirrors and not worth their time. That made it harder for Finney to make any headway in the areas where he preached.

I believe we should pause here for a moment to observe a similar attitude in our day and age. We have all seen "revivals" advertised that did not produce fruit and seemed more man-produced than God-ordained. Our futile attempts to produce revival in the flesh have frustrated the evangelistic efforts of the church. Some wonder if revival and awakening are even possible today. Many are burned out with man-made revivals promoted by aggressive, sensational advertising only to leave the masses feeling disappointed and empty. I'm sure that's exactly the way they felt right before America's Second Great Awakening: burned out and apathetic, wondering if the real thing was even possible anymore.

Hold on! The real thing is coming, my friend! You who are disappointed and disillusioned by the fraudulently-forged, human-driven meetings of the day should know a Third Great Awakening is upon us! The day is quickly approaching when the fulfillment of scripture will manifest: **"For as the waters fill the sea, the earth will be filled with an awareness of the glory of the LORD."** (Hab. 2:14)

Here the phrase**: "The awareness of the glory of the Lord"** stands out to me in bold relief. The day is coming when people will line the streets and suddenly become "**aware**" that the Lord their God has entered the city! Those who were once oblivious to God and His glory will one day be overtaken by His manifest presence. Just as it happened when Daniel Nash prayed the presence of God on Rome, New York we will soon see full cities that were once burned out by religious activity suddenly arrested by divine visitation!

Some today are so burned out that they believe this is no longer possible, but I am fully persuaded that the Lord has saved the best for last. There will be a great harvest of souls before the coming of the Lord.

The same God that brought awakening to America the first two times will move once again a third time. Not only in America but **"as the water fills the sea, <u>the earth</u> will be filled..."** (Hab. 2:14) with people all over the world, recognizing the glory of the Lord for what it is. The earth is groaning for true revival. The harvest is ready to come in and the masses are desperately awaiting their day of deliverance. God is no respecter of persons; what He did before He will do again. The best is yet to come. **Suddenly** Earth shall stand still as the awareness of the Lord's glory comes like waves once again! Bring it on, Lord!

Chapter 3

NASH COULD BE HEARD HALF A MILE AWAY...

"Nash had great confidence in a God who heard and answered prayer. He was not satisfied to stop praying until God answered in mighty power. Praying day and night, great struggling and weakened health were but prices to be paid that God might move in power. The results were opened heavens, glorious power, souls saved, and God glorified. This may well explain why over 80 per cent of Finney's converts

stood without ever backsliding. This may also explain why less than 20 per cent of today's converts last a couple of years." — *J. Paul Reno*

D aniel Nash regularly prayed in private, but he was often so loud that others overheard and were greatly concerned for his welfare. Of course, that was never his intention; it was simply the outpouring of his deeply-impacted soul. In fact, his landlady claimed that wherever he was, even isolated in a far-away room, his fervent prayers nearly shook the house. It's even been said that he could be heard praying as far as a half mile away, (0.804672 km) while secreting himself away in the woods far from town.

Nash was often known to pray especially hard on behalf of those who violently opposed the things of God. In one case, a small-town bar owner was particularly vicious, delighting in using gutter language in the presence of every Christian he could offend. His home even became a haven for others who felt the same way, and together they loudly cursed and railed about the revival that had just come to town.

One of the young converts lived just across the street, and he, in particular, was grievously upset by the man's brutish behavior. The old man exited his house to shout and swear at his neighbor. In fact, the young man could no longer handle the abuse and had seriously considered putting his house on the market, or even giving it away, just to get out of the wicked man's line of sight.

When Father Nash heard someone mention that the man was a hard case, he was deeply grieved for the abuser and immediately took the matter to prayer. Apparently, the issue weighed on him day and night, and he felt led by the Spirit to fervently intercede for the man, according to the will of God. I must again pause for one moment as we gaze into the nature of Daniel Nash. A man who once he carried a burden to intercede for others he prayed until breakthrough happened. This tenacity in prayer I believe he had for Finney up until his death even if he did not attend all the meetings.

Back to our story! Not long afterward, the notorious man stormed into an evening revival meeting, creating quite a stir among those who knew his reputation. Attendees feared that he had come to disturb the proceedings as was his custom. In fact, Christians cowered in the man's presence, and some even got up and left. Finney discerned that the man was in great anguish of mind and no threat. As he watched, the man sat writhing in his seat, clearly very uneasy. He was trembling when he rose and asked to speak. Finney agreed, and the deeply broken man confessed, weeping uncontrollably before the crowd, that he had been critical and abusive toward God and believers regarding revival and everything to do with it.

His confession and radical conversion ultimately shattered the hardness of all hearts within earshot, so that many others also came to Christ, but that was only the beginning. The man went on to change his life entirely, forbidding the use of alcohol and profanities in his former bar, which he turned into a place of prayer. It was only one of many instances where Nash's perseverance in prayer prevailed against all odds and Hell lost another of its generals.

I believe that the coming move of God will crack even the hard cases once again. Do you know any hard cases that are unresponsive and utterly opposed to the Gospel? Daniel Nash targeted these hard cases in special fervent prayer and the Lord stepped in to crack even the hardest of hearts to become soft and receptive to the Gospel. We all know people whom we believe will never change. We may even mark them off our list of possibilities. Yet God is raising up those who will prevail against all odds, and pray fervently for lost souls. The day is coming when hard cases will be so transformed that their testimonies will shake the very foundations of Earth. Dens of iniquity will be transformed into houses of worship and prayer. Many will be astonished at what the Lord will do. He transformed Saul of Tarsus into Paul the Apostle, and His transforming love will chase down others in our day, preparing them for their greatest work yet. Maybe it is a son or daughter or brother or sister, a boss at work, but **don't mark anyone off your list because God is on the move!**

Chapter 4

FULL OF THE POWER OF PRAYER

"The house was as still as death, and most of the people held down their heads. I could see that the young men were agitated. For myself, I regretted that Brother Nash had gone so far. He had committed himself, that God would either take the life of some of them, and send them to Hell, or convert some of them, within a week."

— *Charles Finney on Daniel Nash, his chief intercessor.*

S top for a second and once again consider the phrase that Finney used to describe Father Nash: **"Full of the power of prayer."**

What does that look like? Let your imagination run with that thought for a moment. Try to envision what a person filled with Holy Spirit prayer would sound like. In Nash's case, his anointing was so sweet that those around him couldn't contain their emotions when he prayed. Many wept as he prayed with all that was in him, though outsiders had no idea what he was saying because it was often in a heavenly language.

With united hearts, Finney and Nash prayed that the Holy Spirit would show them the most effective ways to approach lost men. Though they could've come up with man-made ideas, they simply moved and spoke as the Spirit led them, leaving logic and human reasoning behind. In fact, sometimes we are also called, simply to get out of the way and let God move as He pleases because the truth is that He doesn't need our help. He simply requires yielded empty vessels through which He can move.

Both men believed in the power of prayer, knowing that nothing would happen without it. In order to receive the truth, people had to be able to hear with the ears of the Spirit the anointed Word. **Faith comes by hearing, and hearing by the Word of God (Romans 10:17).**

So, several weeks before some evangelistic crusades, Father Nash would slip quietly into the town to seek out like-minded locals to join him in prayer. Then the prayer team would hide away to fervently pray down the power of God for Finney's upcoming crusade. This is exactly why people oftentimes fell upon the sidewalks in repentance before ever joining one of the meetings!

Intercession. Fervent intercession. Winning souls depends on it!

This is an intriguing note from Charles Finney's journal: **"On one occasion when I got to town to start a Revival, a lady contacted me who ran a boarding house. She said, 'Brother Finney, do you know a Father Nash? He and two other men have been at my boarding house for the last three days, but they haven't eaten a bite of food. I opened the door and peeped in at them because I could hear them groaning, and I saw**

them lying down on their faces. They're been this way for three days, lying prostrate on the floor and groaning. I thought something awful must have happened to them. I was afraid to go in and I didn't know what to do. Would you please come see them?' 'No, it isn't necessary,' Finney replied. 'They just have a spirit of travailing in prayer.'"

By the time Charles Finney opened the meetings and began to preach, Father Nash (and sometimes Rev. Clary) had already been pouring out their heart in gut-wrenching prayer, believing and declaring what God had already promised: that the spirit of conviction and repentance would fall on all those in attendance, and that's exactly what happened!

Think of how effective Mr. Finney's preaching must have been when fueled by that kind of fervent prayer! Turbo-preaching indeed, inspired by fire shut up in his bones! But things weren't always rosy on the evangelistic trail. Mr. Finney wrote about one particular incident that stood out in his mind:

"A number of young men stood blocking the team's evangelical work. Both Finney and Father Nash resolved to overcome this obstacle by the power of prayer, and so they did until they felt confident that no power in Hell or on Earth could stop the revival.

"Father Nash, normally a quiet man, arose in a nearly filled meeting-house and addressed that group of men who were resisting the revival. Father Nash pointed out the guilt and danger of the course those men were taking and said to them, 'Now, mark me, young men! God will break your ranks in less than one week, either by converting you or by sending some of you to Hell.' For emphasis, he slapped the pew and rocked it resoundingly with a power beyond his limbs. Father Nash then dropped into a seat and groaned in pain.

"Tuesday morning of that same week, the leader of that band of men went to Charles Finney in distress. He was prepared to accept Christ and he broke down before Mr. Finney like a child, confessed and gave himself to the Lord. The new convert said, 'What shall I do, Mr. Finney?' Finney replied, 'Go immediately to all your young companions and pray with them and exhort them at once to turn to the Lord.' Before the week was out, nearly all (if not all) of that group of men were hoping in Christ."

The importance of Father Nash's prayer ministry to Finney's work was immeasurable. Daniel Nash preferred to work on the sidelines, rarely stepping into the limelight, providing a prayerful pathway for the Lord to rain down His power and grace on entire communities, often at huge expense to his physical health.

Together, Charles Finney and Daniel Nash did more to spearhead revival than any other team in American history. In the end, the Dream Team led a revival in Rochester, New York, where it is believed that over 100,000 souls accepted Jesus Christ as their Lord and Savior.

In our day, we can begin to see the start of a fivefold ministry working together in unity according to their divine purpose. These are men and women of God who do not carry an orphan spirit that are threatened by other ministries. Where there is no competition and the leaders of God emerge together working according to their specific calling. They know who their Father is and therefore honor and esteem others higher than themselves. (Romans 12:10) We have seen the day where many seek fame and fortune at any cost and where those who haven't been called by God do it anyway because they want positions of power and notoriety.

Much like the disciples who argued with each other about which one of them was the greatest, we see many who want to rule in places of importance and have others serve them. **They use people for the ministry rather than using their ministry for the people.** Our Father is raising up a new breed of leader now who will use the power of the towel to serve others even as Christ did in John 13, where the very King of all Kings knelt down to wash the feet of others ... even a traitor! This new leader will come with a towel and esteem others more than himself.

Charles Finney and Daniel Nash are prototypes of a divinely-inspired prayer team ordained by God who work together according to the dictates of the Holy Spirit. They will spearhead revival fire in the next Great Awakening and the people will be astonished at the honor and humility in which they operate.

Depths of Prayer

"I was acquainted with an individual who used to keep a list of persons for whom he was especially concerned;

and I have had the opportunity to know a multitude of persons, for whom he became thus interested, who were immediately converted. I have seen him pray for persons on his list when he was literally in an agony for them; and have sometimes known him call on some other person to help him pray for such-a-one. I have known his mind to fasten thus on an individual of hardened, abandoned character, and who could not be reached in an ordinary way." — **Charles Finney on Daniel Nash, his chief intercessor.**

Not many of us stay awake all night, fasting and praying, weeping, or shivering in the cold, unaware of our surroundings because we're in such deep communion with God.

What would lead us into such depths of prayer? Crushing debt? A medical report? A divorce looming just over the horizon? Someone we love near death? I submit to you that such things are momentary. Tragic, yes, but passing nonetheless.

I'm not being insensitive when I say that. I'm saying that these events simply do not have the power to sustain us enduringly in the depth of prayer that deeply stirs the Holy Spirit.

"Jesus said unto him, Thou shalt **love the Lord** thy God with **all thy heart, and with all thy soul, and with all thy mind**" (Matt. 22:37, emphasis mine).

Only love for God and compassion for others can sustain that depth of fervent prayer—the kind that brings us to tears and leads us to fasting, blocking out everything else.

How can that level of love be manifest in our prayers? Many believers pose such questions without understanding that the kind of love Jesus speaks of here is unequalled, which is why scripture says that many are called, but few are chosen. The sad truth is that few of us are willing to lay down our lives to such an extent, even for the purpose of winning lost souls.

At this point, I believe the only one way to get to this place is by loving others as we love ourselves. Jesus explains this concept in Matthew 22:39:

"The second most important commandment is like this one. And it is 'Love others as much as you love yourself.'"

So, the goal is:

a) To stir the Holy Spirit, we have to pray with complete conviction and abandon.

b) To be able to sustain prayer with complete conviction and abandon, we must love the Lord with all our hearts, minds, and souls.

c) To be able to love the Lord with ALL our hearts, minds, and souls, we must intercede on the behalf of others.

d) To be able to intercede for others, we must love others more than we love ourselves.

There it is. Intercession, praying for others, which is **only accomplished through the grace of the Holy Spirit.**

Chapter 5

THE ANXIOUS SEAT

> *"A revival may be expected when Christians have a spirit of prayer for a revival. That is, when they pray as if their hearts were set upon it. When Christians have the spirit of prayer for a revival. When they go about groaning out their hearts desire. When they have real travail of soul."* – **Charles Finney**

As a praying man himself, Finney was well aware of the great power of prayer. In reality, it was the foundation of his ministry and key to his profound success. In each new town, he met with those in authority and scheduled meeting times. There he preached every weekday evening and three times on Sunday in a wooden structure that scarcely accommodated the crowds. One day, a woman of great influence asked to speak to him, expressing concern over her soul, yet unwilling to give up her worldly ways. After her meeting with Finney, she was greatly convicted of sin and surrendered herself to Christ, which completely transformed her life. As a result, this high-society woman invited everyone she knew to the revival. Some people came from as far as 100 miles (161 km) away to hear the Gospel.

Finney was always asking God for new ways to minister to the lost, and for the first time, while in Rochester, he reserved the first several rows so that those who responded to the first altar call in history could come forward to be ministered to by those who could lead them to Christ. Just like any new measure, his new methods were loudly criticized, at least until the results spoke for themselves. Then, once the criticism died down, those new measures became the pattern for revivals for the next 100 years!

One evening, a husband and wife entered the revival, already under great conviction, afraid for the future of their souls. However, neither of them was ready to go forward for fear of what the other would say. The next day, the wife went to see Finney, saying she wouldn't accept Christ because her husband would not. She said that if he was going to Hell, she wanted to be with him there. When her husband told her he was going forward to sit in the first row, also known as the **anxious seat**, she said she wasn't going to the meeting because she had no intention of watching as he left her behind. However, when it came time for the meeting, she sneaked into the back pew to watch and broke down in conviction and went to the altar, though neither of them saw the other and neither felt they had gotten a breakthrough once it was over.

The following morning, they both went to see Finney alone, without knowing the other was there. Sensing that the Spirit of God was moving, Finney beckoned them to come together where they finally got the breakthrough they sought and were gloriously saved, filled with peace and incredible joy in the Lord. It was a remarkable thing to see: a humble man of God who was willing to spend endless hours warring beside lost souls. In the end, it is said that no single individual had more influence than Charles Finney, and the secret weapon behind all of this was the fervent prayers of Nash and others!

Rochester, NY

"They used to complain," Finney penned in his Memoirs in reference to theology-educated ministers, "that I let down the dignity of the pulpit; that I was a dis grace to the ministerial profession; that I talked like a lawyer at the bar; that I talked to the people in a colloquial manner; that I said 'you' instead of preaching about sin and sinners and saying 'they'; that I said 'hell' and with such emphasis as often to shock the people." – **Charles Finney, The Memoirs of the Rev. Charles G. Finney (New York: A. S. Barnes and Company, 1876), p. 83.**

Rochester, New York was the site of the greatest outpouring of Charles Finney's preaching career. It began in September of 1830, and the city was completely transformed in a matter of six months as a result. Even his greatest critics had to admit it was the greatest revival that the world had ever seen, bringing an estimated 100,000 souls to salvation. Converts included people from all walks of life, from the lowest to the highest echelons of society, and they shut down bars and houses of prostitution as well as every other ungodly business in the area. The crime rate took a precipitous nosedive, leaving law enforcement officers with almost nothing to do. It inspired revivals in many other places as people arrived who were saved and then went home to share the Gospel with others. It even became the pattern for every other revival from that time until now.

Incredibly it happened almost by accident. Finney initially declined the invitation sent by the Third Presbyterian Church, whose congregation was without a pastor and in danger of closing entirely. He believed it to be a very risky proposition because of the infighting between three of the town's churches, the area's pathetic moral condition, and the lack of a local pastor. However, the Holy Spirit evidently believed otherwise because He continued to nudge Finney to reconsider. Finney even made a list of reasons why he shouldn't preach there, but the Holy

Spirit argued that because of the problems, those people needed that message more than anyone else!

The following morning, Finney notified his team that they were going to Rochester, only this trip was different because he would be accompanied by his family and two dear and faithful friends and prayer warriors, Rev. Daniel Nash and Rev. Abel B. Clary. Their strategy wasn't as complicated as today; it consisted of only two parts, prevailing prayer and powerful preaching. For years, Finney himself had honed his skills as an evangelist, while Nash and Clary had become experts at giving themselves over to fervent prayer, seeking an open heaven to pour out on the revival to come.

As was their custom, the prayer warriors arrived several days early, rented a room where they isolated themselves from distractions and began to pray for the city, without regard for comfort, sleep or food. They were rarely seen because they almost never left that prayer cell. They fasted for days, lying prostrate on the cold, hard floor of their tiny unheated room and simply prayed, wept and wailed, believing God would finish what the Holy Spirit inspired.

Today, the church has gone off the tracks and has made soul winning a business, with a man-made business plan that essentially gives all the credit to man, instead of simply praying, waiting on God and believing for a great outcome, knowing it can only happen by the power of the Holy Spirit. Scripture says, **"Not by might, not by power, but by My Spirit, says the Lord."** (Zechariah 4:6) Clearly, God needs us to be clean vessels willing to come alongside Him and go the distance to change the world.

Finney's routine seldom varied. He would vehemently preach the unadulterated truth, raging against sin and holding up the Bible as the one and only authoritative Word of God, then invite sinners to come forward and sit in the front rows where his support staff would minister for as long as it took for people to respond to the call for salvation. As mentioned, in that day, they called those rows *the anxious seat*, while today it's known as an altar call. The truth is that he inspired the converts to leave the world behind and seek holiness like never before. That call to live a holy life inspired the holiness movement of the nineteenth century and the twentieth century's charismatic movement.

Finney was one of the first to include behind-the-scenes prayer meetings before and during his services. He also made a habit of holding meetings for weeks at a time and never ended services without an altar call because that was, after all, the point. He also instituted the push for decisions from those sitting in the front before allowing them to leave the auditorium. Those methods influenced other great evangelists of their time, including D. L. Moody, Billy Sunday, and Billy Graham.

In the end, it's vital to realize that revival isn't a spontaneous event. While it may come suddenly, it never comes by accident. Rather, it is the result of godly people pressing until something happens in the spirit. It's time we once again got down to the business of fervent prayer and preaching without apology, if we want to see moves that occurred in Finney's day.

Our cities are hurting and their people are dying, lost forever to the fires of Hell. Do we care? Does it shake us to the core to even imagine it? If not, we too need revival to break our hardened hearts and allow God to replace our hearts of stone with empathy and compassion.

The Lord is searching for those who will carry His words and His vision in their hearts. With a holy fire on their lips, they will speak His heart to a spiritually famished generation. Hungry lovers of God are desperate to hear the Word of the Lord. They want His heart to be communicated to them.

Then the LORD touched my mouth and said, "See, I have put my words in your mouth!" (Jer. 1: 9, NLT)

"Now go, and do as I have told you. I will help you speak well, and I will tell you what to say" (Ex. 4:12, NLT).

In the end times, there will be some who will prefer to "sermonize" rather than "wait on Him" for "divine bread" from Heaven. It's far easier to pull a message off the Internet or from a book than to seek earnestly for fresh manna. We can certainly learn from others, but when our messages lack substance and anointing because we did not seek Him first, God is saddened and we are shortchanged. We need the true manna from Heaven He wants to give us that will actually transform hearts! He desires to fill our mouths with the thoughts of His heart for that particular moment in time. When ministers cease to get real messages from God, their sermons become empty and heartless.

The true Word of the Lord will shake up Satan's kingdom and tear down religious strongholds. Bondages will break and chains will fall. Spirit and life will provide spiritual substance to the hungry and desperate. God is raising up people like Charles Finney who care more about what God thinks than what people think; a man or woman who will hold nothing back and refuse to tickle the ears of the listener. They will carry the Word of the Lord with power and presence. Let me say this again. **It's time we once again got down to the business of fervent prayer and preaching without apology, if we want to see the kind of God's moves that occurred in Finney's day!**

Chapter 6

THE TOWN WAS FULL OF PRAYER! COULD IT HAPPEN TODAY?

"In this state of things, Brother Nash and myself (Finney), after consultation, made up our minds that that thing must be overcome by prayer, and that it could not be reached in any other way. We therefore retired to a grove and gave ourselves to prayer until we prevailed, and we felt confident that no power which Earth or Hell could interpose, would be allowed permanently to stop the revival."
— **Charles Finney on Daniel Nash, his chief intercessor.**

At this point you're probably asking what Nash did to be such a powerful prayer warrior. Could it happen today? Could mighty prayer actually transform a city even now? I mentioned earlier that this was indeed possible and is coming. What can God do with a few prayer warriors who know how to pull Heaven down to Earth for such a time as this? The story of Rome, New York, and the sheriff's conversion testify to the transforming power of fervent intercession that occurred in Daniel Nash's life.

Fervent prayer was the secret to the city's incredible transformation in Nash's day and is still true today. As we mentioned earlier that before Charles Finney ever stepped into town, in some meetings Daniel Nash had already arrived to storm Heaven as if his life depended on it. From dark, damp rented cellars to tiny hidden meeting rooms, his anguished voice could be heard endlessly crying out for the lost souls of the region. Tears, trembling, and groaning filled the space until those within earshot grew concerned and were compelled to check on Nash. In the end, his prayers were so powerful that Heaven couldn't refuse to move on his behalf. Here are more thoughts from Charles Finney who said this of Daniel Nash:

"I have known people who prayed till they were soaked in sweat on a cold winter's day. I have known people who have prayed for hours until they were totally drained of strength because of the agony of their souls. I have worked with a man of this caliber."

From that point on, the revival couldn't be contained and it spread like wildfire, becoming a mighty move of the Spirit, much like what happened at Pentecost. Mr. Finney wrote that villagers and those farther afield felt awestruck at the tangible presence of God—even unbelievers realized that something amazing was happening around them. In fact, the county sheriff made his home in Utica but often traveled to a nearby town called Rome where he stayed overnight while conducting business. While he had heard about the revival, he didn't believe it could change things so radically. He and others even laughed about it until he had to make a trip to Rome. He was glad for the chance to see for himself whether or not the news was true.

On the way, he was thinking of nothing in particular until he crossed the bridge over an old canal located a mile or so from town. It was then that he felt something change: it was like God's presence had filled the entire atmosphere. He was indeed awestruck by the sensation and, no matter what, he couldn't escape that awareness. What's more, the impression only grew stronger as he approached his destination. When he arrived at the hotel, a man came to take care of his horse. The man said not a word but, like himself, was apparently afraid to speak at all.

Inside the hotel, he found the man he was to meet, but the presence of God was so powerful that they could scarcely attend to business. He himself was so struck by the power that he had to rush from the table several times and run to the window to keep from weeping out loud. From all appearances, the power had the exact same effect on everyone else as well. After hurrying to complete his business, he returned home, never again speaking lightly of the power of God. He had never in all his life been so impacted, and it changed him forever, so that he gave his heart to Christ within a couple of weeks.

The work of the Spirit had done its job and changed everyone and everything in its path so much that no one wanted it to stop. They held sunrise prayer meetings that continued for over a year, no matter the season. People often said that the town bore no resemblance whatsoever to the place it once was. Whatever sinful behavior remained had to hide itself because no overt sin was tolerated without confrontation for even a moment. The streets became impromptu prayer meeting sites among two or three residents, who would begin to pray at a moment's notice over any situation. **They often focused their corporate prayer on those still unconverted, until there were no unbelievers left among them.**

The life-changing revival spread until it involved Utica, New York, where it headquartered in the area's largest hotel. Untold numbers were saved there, after merely stopping for a meal or a night's stay and becoming mightily convicted. Over time it was said that no one could pass through the town without being forever touched by the power of God. The truth is that it would take an entire book to describe the incredible things that happened because of the fervent prayers of Daniel Nash.

Scripture says that God is the same yesterday, to-day, and forever. If that is so, He still responds to the fervent prayers of His children today, but are we willing to pay the price to change our little corner of the world? Oh, Lord, let it be so!

PRAYER CHANGES THINGS!

Before I close this chapter, I want you to focus on these key words: **"They often focused their corporate prayer on those still unconverted, until there were no unbelievers left among them."**

Did you catch that? **"<u>Until there were no unbelievers left among them</u>!"** Can you imagine having a prayer movement so explosive that no single unsaved individual was left in the whole town? Is this even possible? Will this happen again or is this just a one-time event?

We know God is raising up a remnant of reapers like Finney to carry the burden for the lost. **"Thrust in your sickle and reap, for the time has come for You to reap for the harvest of the Earth is ripe"** (Rev. 14; 15).

This scripture speaks of the 'Son of Man' being the Reaper. The sickle is "a reaping hook" harvest instrument. In a very real sense, the evangelist who goes forth in the calling of the Master is also reaping the "precious fruit of the earth." In the hands of the evangelist (the sent one), the reaping hook is The Word of God preached forcefully with such authority and might in the power of the Spirit to harvest souls for the Kingdom.

Ever since the fall of man, even after God's great flood of judgment, people on Earth have progressively degenerated and traveled far afield from the Father's dream of us as a family. Humankind is still hopelessly entangled with the cunning and deceitful "destroyer." We persistently engage in ongoing rebellion by following after other gods disguised in the trappings of wealth and status, human reasoning, and self-indulgence. Despite the enormity of this mass defiance of His created ones, God devised an effective plan.

Over and over the compassionate, long-suffering Creator has called us back, pleading with us, "not willing that any should perish." **Jesus came! Jesus**

restored! Jesus conquered! Jesus commissioned!

The prime agents of God's steady pursuit of His human creation have been the evangelists. Various meanings of the word "evangelist" have included apostle, clergyman, messengers, etc. Indeed, evangelism is said to be one of the highest of divine callings. This "reaching out" was authorized by our Lord Jesus Christ. It was He who commissioned his disciples to **"Go into all the world and preach the gospel to every creature–beginning in Jerusalem." "...repentance and remission of sins should be preached in His name to all nations, beginning at Jerusalem"** (Mark 16:15 – Luke 24:47).

And go they did! Over the centuries, treading the landscapes of the world's lost, a consecrated army of selfless men and women have courageously battled for the Kingdom of God. These faithful pioneers passed the Gospel torch lit by the Master Himself to following generations. Charles Finney and Daniel Nash preached and prayed in the harvest, in a prayer movement so powerful that it has seldom occurred again. We're living in a day where we should also focus our corporate prayer on those still unconverted until there are no unbelievers left among us! Today, God is raising up a prayer movement like none other! Can you see it? Can you hear the fervent prayers echoing from unfamiliar places?

Chapter 7

ABEL CLARY: CHAMPION OF FERVENT PRAYER

Clary could scarcely speak when he said, "Pray, Brother Finney." Finney knelt beside his bed and prayed for lost souls and continued to pray until Clary's distress passed as he lay there, utterly exhausted and spent. — **Charles Finney on Abel Clary, his chief intercessor.**

T he late summer's early morning sun was just sneaking over the horizon when I climbed into my Nissan to make the much anticipated two-hour journey from Rochester, New York to the Adams Rural Cemetery located in Adams, New York. The town of Adams is located in Jefferson County, south of Watertown, and was named after President John Adams.

Ironically, Charles Finney also had roots in Adams when he joined the congregation of George Washington Gale and became director of the church choir. After a dramatic conversion to the Lord and baptism into the Holy Spirit, he left his legal practice to preach the Gospel of Jesus Christ. However, when you study the names of well-known citizens connected with the town of Adams, there is a glaring absence of one notable name: **The Rev. Abel B. Clary.**

Try as I might, I couldn't dig up much information on the great man of God, but this book would not be complete if I didn't mention and give honor to this amazing man of prayer and his special relationship with Father Daniel Nash. Little is known about the personal life of Daniel Nash, but even less is known about Abel Clary.

Here is what we do know: Rev. Abel B. Clary was born June 17, 1796, in Colrain, Mass., to Abel Clary Sr. and Dolly Baker Clary. (Some sources suggest that he was born in Conway, Mass., thirty-six miles from Colrain.)

He died Jan. 1, 1833, at the young age of 37, just two years shy of the end of the Second Great Awakening. He was buried off South Main Street in the Adams Rural Cemetery, Adams, Jefferson County, New York. We know his parents outlived him. His Father Abel Clary Sr. was born in 1763 and passed away at the mature age of 90 on September 20, 1853. His Mother Dolly Clary was born in 1767 and passed away on July 29, 1843 at the age of 76. Both his parents were also buried at the Adams Rural Cemetery, Adams, Jefferson County, New York. I am sure his parents were deeply grieved that their son died before them. I believe to lose a child is the very worst pain a parent can face, I felt so sad for Abel Sr. who lost his son and wife before him.

From my research I could find no records of marriage or any children the Rev Abel B Clary left behind, so there's a good chance he never married. We know that he had an amazing relationship with Father Nash as they combined their passion for lost souls. These two dear men of God were the chief forerunners of Evangelist Charles Finney. They were desperate for souls to be saved from eternal Hell, and their fervent prayers actually birthed a great awakening that, in the end, turned the world upside down. On their knees, they prayed until the damp, dark prayer cellars were aflame with the very fire of the Holy Spirit.

Author Leonard Ravenhill tells the following story: **"I met an old lady who told me a story about Charles Finney that has challenged me over the years. Finney went to Bolton to minister,**

but before he began, two men knocked on the door of her humble cottage, wanting lodging. The poor woman looked amazed, for she had no extra accommodations. Finally, for about twenty-five cents a week, the two men, none other than Fathers Nash and Clary, rented a dark and damp cellar for the period of the Finney meetings (at least two weeks), and there in that self-chosen cell, those prayer partners battled the forces of darkness."

Today I believe Abel Clary represents a prophetic message to the church regarding the vital need for **"fervent prayer support."** As we know, Scripture says that where two or three get together to pray, their power is mighty.

"Again, truly I tell you that if two of you on Earth agree about anything they ask for, it will be done for them by my Father in heaven" (Matt. 18:19).

It is rare today to find two such men who are willing to lay it all down to give themselves over to birthing a revival through unity and fervent intercession. They had no agenda other than to lift their voices in one accord, believing for a spiritual awakening in their day. They made no effort to build up a ministry or develop a brand, and no one took credit for the power of God that fell; they were just two humble men who partnered up to link their hearts in beautiful harmony with the Spirit of God.

Charles Finney said that Clary continued to pray as long as Finney was preaching and never stopped until after the evangelist left the area. Clary did not appear in public often but gave himself utterly to prayer. He humbly accepted the assignment to pray Heaven down to Earth, so that the lost would be convicted and subsequently find Christ. In fact, Finney only discovered Clary's prayer journal after the man went to be with the Lord. In its pages, he had chronicled the heavy burdens that God inspired him to pray for. Looking at it from this vantage point, we can see how those urges to pray lined up exactly with the outpourings of the Spirit that occurred so often during Finney's powerful meetings.

Finney's journal described Abel Clary as the son of a very excellent man, who, at that time, was an elder in the church where Finney accepted Christ. Clary's father apparently came to Christ during the same set of revival services where Finney himself had been converted. Abel was licensed to preach, but the burden to pray was so heavy that he could scarcely stand, let alone speak or preach. So, he chose to remain behind the scenes, lending all his efforts to prayer with the goal of allowing access to the Holy Spirit to transform the hearts of men. His soul was so deeply affected during prayer that he would often writhe and groan in anguish for the lost souls of men. He was apparently a man of few words, which is often the case with those who have a mighty fiery burden to pray.

Finney went on to say that he had never met Abel Clary until a visitor asked if he knew a minister by the name of Mr. Abel B. Clary. When he answered that he had no knowledge of the man, his guest told him he was currently staying at his home and had been there for some time; then he admitted that he didn't know what to make of the man. Finney said he hadn't seen him at any of their meetings, and the man said he wouldn't be able to go because he spent nearly every hour of the day and night in such mental agony that all he could do was pray for revival. The guest went on to describe the way he would groan and pray, lying prostrate on the floor, unaware of anyone or anything going on around him at the time. Finney immediately realized that God had sent the man to cover his meetings in prayer, which was why the miraculous had become the norm there. He sent the visitor on his way, telling him not to worry, that everything would turn out as it should.

Finney's journal focused on one very notable event. During the time he was preaching in Auburn, he recognized Abel Clary in a rare meeting and noticed that he seemed to be heavily burdened to pray right then and there. Finney, who was well aware of the man's reputation as a powerful prayer warrior, was glad to have him there. His brother, Dr. Clary, was also a professor of religion but had none of his brother's gifts for prayer. During a break between services, the doctor invited Finney to join them for lunch and a rest. Once they arrived at the house, it wasn't long before they were called to come and eat. Dr. Clary turned to his brother and asked him to bless the food, and he nodded that he would. However, he had scarcely spoken a word before he broke down, pushed his chair away from the table, and fled to his room. The doctor, who assumed he was feeling ill, followed him, only to return a moment later to tell Finney that Abel wanted to see him. When Finney asked what was wrong, he answered that he didn't know but that his brother appeared to be in great distress. He thought it was his state of mind that upset him so deeply.

When Finney arrived at his room, Clary lay groaning on his bed, and the evangelist realized that he was seeing evidence of the Spirit making an intercession for him, with groaning that couldn't be uttered, exactly as described in Scripture (Rom. 8:26). Momentarily, Clary could scarcely speak when he said, "Pray, Brother Finney." Finney knelt beside his bed and prayed for lost souls and continued to pray until Clary's distress passed as he lay there, utterly exhausted and spent. Then Finney joined those at the table, amazed by what had happened. He knew that he had witnessed the voice of God, praying through Abel Clary, and he was convinced that God would use it in a powerful way. That's exactly what happened. The pastor of the church hosting the revival later reported that over the six weeks he was preaching, 500 people had come to know the Lord. Amazing!

Few people have ever heard of Reverend Abel B. Clary, but his humble, sweet spirit and willingness to fervently pray are responsible for the salvation of many souls in his day. Knowing that God often demands great sacrifice in order to produce great results, how will we respond? When the Holy Spirit calls on us to fervently pray, will we be willing to set aside distractions, to get down to the business of prayer? If we won't, who will?

I believe God is raising up forerunners like Abel Clary who know how to sustain revival through supportive prayer. This special brand of intercessor doesn't care about name recognition or being seen on camera praying. You will find them in a back room somewhere birthing another great awakening through fervent intercession. They groan and travail, carrying a burden that far surpasses the natural realm. Others may misunderstand them, but their fervent prayers shake nations.

With a plan to visit the cemetery where Abel B. Clary was buried, I pulled into Adams with great anticipation that morning. I'd been communing with the Lord on the road, and I felt sure there was a special purpose for the powerful presence of God that accompanied me that day. I turned onto Main Street and found myself right in front of the Adams Rural Cemetery. From my car, I prayed out loud, "Where should I go, Holy Spirit?" I had no idea where this great man of God and his family were buried. I drove about halfway into the cemetery and gently pulled my car over. I got out and began walking in search of the right grave marker. I pulled my phone out, looking at pictures of the tombstones of his family, searching for any clue as to their whereabouts. After about an hour I circled back around near where I parked my car and walked down another path and still I couldn't find the burial plots. I paused, closed my eyes, and cried out, "Father, please tell me where their plots are located and order my steps." I opened my eyes and looked up to see the burial plots of Rev. Abel B. Clary and his beloved parents, Abel Clary Sr. and Dolly Clary. I was surprised and overjoyed to see that the tombstones were located directly in line with my car! God was all over this visit!

I struggled to hold back the tears as I stood at the gravesite pausing to ponder and celebrate the short life of Rev. Abel B. Clary, who was part of a special family known for prayer and their passionate love for God. At the top of his parents' tombstone was a picture of the Word of God. Oh, how they must have loved His Holy Word! I could only marvel at the incredible legacy they must have imparted to their children. These days, we can scarcely imagine what God can do with a family dedicated to fervent prayer and intercession.

That morning, I stood alone in that cemetery, but I wasn't really alone. The Lord was with me, stirring up deep wells of prayer inside me. I released fervent prayers for Rochester—my city—for yet another great awakening. I was overwhelmed, awed to honor that great family, realizing what an incredible gift they had been to the body of Christ. I thanked God for them and knew that if God could use the prayer life of Abel Clary to change the course of American history, He can use those of us who live now to fervently pray for another mighty move of God. *Lord, start with us!* The Spirit and the Bride say, "Come, Holy Spirit and pour out on us again!" The name of Abel Clary may not have been recorded in his town's historical records, but Heaven knows his name and wants him to be a model of the power of fervent prayer and intercession that we can emulate today!

Chapter 8

NO POWER WITHOUT PRAYER

"If the presence of God is in the church, the church will draw the world in. If the presence of God is not in the church, the world will draw the church out." **– Charles Finney**

"How often God visited the Jewish Church with judgments because they would not repent and be revived at the call of His prophets! How often have we seen Churches, and even whole denominations, cursed with a curse, because they would not wake up and seek the Lord." **– Charles Finney**

The outpouring was so great that not one in the crowd could stand or stay in his seat, or even hold his head up as he lay on the floor, stricken by the power of the Living God.

C harles Finney had a reputation as a powerful evangelist whose sermons were like lightning that flashed conviction into even the hardest of hearts. Though he spoke using simple terms that even a child could understand, his prayers were deep, bringing Heaven to Earth with declarations and decrees right out of God's Word. He also had an unusual way of judging sin while showing mercy with tears to even the vilest of sinners. He was clearly a voice of prophecy that transformed the world of his day.

While most evangelists chose to minister in places that welcomed the Gospel, Finney went to areas considered impenetrable to the Gospel message, believing that was where the Gospel was most needed. Books about Finney are filled with stories of supernatural manifestations of the Spirit that couldn't be disputed. One story in particular tells of how he was preaching in a schoolhouse when suddenly a great weight of conviction fell on the audience, so that, one by one, they tumbled from their seats and lay prostrate on the floor, weeping and begging God for mercy.

He was so anointed by the Holy Spirit that people often felt conviction before he ever spoke a single word. All they had to do was look at him to be confronted by the reality of their own sin. On one occasion he had just been taken on a tour of a large factory in Utica, New York when one and then another of the workers fell under conviction, even though he said not a word. The majority of workers there were lying on the floor, so that those in charge stopped the machinery while Finney led them to the Lord.

Can you imagine carrying such an anointing that full crowds fall under the weight of conviction just by being in the presence of a Spirit-filled person? I'm sure Finney's intent was not to show this off in a flashy way but instead walk in humility, convinced that the power lies with prayer warriors like Daniel Nash and Abel Clary. These humble men were praying in the Holy Spirit outpouring by the minute. At that time, the very soul of New York was the focus of a mighty spiritual battle, which we believe is exactly why God chose these three humble men to war in the spirit.

It was said that Charles Finney carried such a manifest presence as he spoke that he was careful not to raise his voice prematurely, so people didn't fall under the power too early in the meeting. He even learned to control the modulation of his voice under the power of the Spirit! What an anointing! As the result of intense prayer efforts, Finney's preaching had a greater impact than most people had ever seen or even heard of. Even Finney himself admitted that such power came because of an unusual secret weapon—the ongoing intercession for souls, literally praying without ceasing with his friends and like-minded locals. As a result, miracles and healings became the norm, and many people attended just to see it for themselves. Though they had come out of curiosity, most of them left transformed by the power of God, never to be the same again.

I also believe God sent Nash and Clary to prayerfully erect a wall of protection around Finney's meetings, for they had inspired fierce spiritual and physical warfare that included overt ridicule and even acts of violence. As we know, great outpourings stir the enemy into a frenzy and he will always do whatever it takes to prevent people from coming to Christ. In the case of the Oneida New York meetings, the opposing forces actually hanged an effigy of Mr. Finney. They also gathered around the house of God and rained down stones against the building and even discharged guns through the windows, effectively hindering listeners from hearing the Gospel. Yet, despite every kind of opposition, the move of God could not be stopped. In fact, the more the opposition grew the greater the outpouring became.

As the opposition watched this enigma progress, the fear of the Lord fell upon those who dared "touch God's anointed." At one particular meeting, an atheist stood and began criticizing Finney and his teachings. He continued to blaspheme and curse the services and the congregation, who immediately went into deep travailing and prayer, until the man left a short time later. Even after his departure, the Spirit held sway, as the people wept, grieving in the Spirit for the lost man. The following morning, they discovered that the man had died in his sleep.

During Finney's evangelist meetings in Evans Mills, there lived a man who hated the Gospel and regularly blasphemed the Scriptures. Outside every meeting he could be seen shouting and swearing, refusing to attend. After an evening of disrupting the meetings, he fell off his chair at breakfast and his family called the doctor, who told him he was dying, and if he had anything to say, he'd better get to it. In the end, he had only enough strength to say, "Don't let Finney pray over my corpse." After the man's death, all opposition ceased and the meetings flourished with magnificent outpourings and many souls saved.

In spite of the efforts to hinder the outpouring, it was like a wildfire that couldn't be contained or stopped and spread from city to city, according to the mighty move of the Spirit. Wherever Finney was preaching, the Holy Spirit moved as never before. He was steadfastly preaching the importance of holiness in the life of a true believer. He couldn't resist telling it like it is, and people responded to the simple truth that if they didn't repent, they'd spend eternity in Hell without remedy. And repent they did. An estimated quarter million souls gave their hearts to

Christ during that time, turning their little corner of the world upside down.

It's easy to feel sentimental about "the good old days", but in this case, it should be something we seek after today: living holy, preaching the untarnished truth, letting the chips fall where they may, and wooing people with tender love and compassion because we care. It seems only a remnant of preachers today have God's priorities in mind and refuse to tickle the ears of the audience so they don't lose support, which must be heartbreaking to God. It's not about money, power, fame, or a name but about the eternal destiny of lost souls for whom we will give an account.

In our day we've been blessed to have among us powerful people of God who refuse to compromise. David Wilkerson and Steve Hill quickly come to mind as men who preached and wrote the marvelous truth of the Gospel during their lifetimes that will affect generations to come in Jesus' name.

During the revival at Evans Mills, Finney based his sermon on the Scripture in Genesis 24:49:

"Now if you will deal kindly and truly with my master, tell me. And if not, tell me, that I might turn to the right or the left."

Finney's preaching was like the thunder of Heaven, piercing the hearts of the lost, so that they couldn't resist the wooing of the Holy Spirit who moved in visible ways that no one could argue. When he finished preaching, he said that now they knew the truth, the ball was in their court and they could never return to their previous ignorance. He went on to say that if they chose not to follow Christ, they could blame no one but themselves when they were eternally separated from God. It was a radical new slant on things. Though most people of that day attended church on a regular basis, few had actually been confronted with the truth—that they were in desperate need of a Savior. As a result of Finney's preaching and the behind-the-scenes fervent prayers of Nash and Clary, those faithful churchgoers became passionate followers and disciples of Jesus Christ.

The following is a quote from Finney's altar call:

"Those who are now willing to pledge to me and to Christ that you will immediately make your peace with God, please rise up...you who are committed to remain in your present attitude, not to accept Christ please remain seated." They looked at one another and remained seated. Finney then said, "Then you are committed, you have rejected Christ and His Gospel. You are witnesses one against the other, and God is witness against you all. You may remember as long as you live that you have thus publicly committed yourselves against the Savior, saying, 'We will not have this Man to reign over us.' (Luke 19:14) The congregation then rose up in anger and started to leave. Finney then stopped talking and they paused and looked back at him. He said, "I am sorry for you and will preach to you but once more...tomorrow night."

Once the service ended, everyone left, except one weeping deacon who grabbed Finney's hand. He said the people would be back because God wasn't through dealing with them yet. He told Finney not to be discouraged because the Holy Spirit wouldn't let them rest or leave things as they were. The following night the church was standing room only, and the service hadn't even begun when the Spirit began to move. Finney began speaking, using the text in Isaiah 2:10-11:

"Say to the righteous that it shall be well with them, for they shall eat the fruit of their doings. Woe to the wicked! It shall be ill with them, for the rewards of his hands shall be given him."

As a result, the masses were moved by the Spirit with such power that it was like a firing squad had opened fire, piercing the division of soul and spirit. The outpouring was so great **that not one in the crowd could stand or stay in his seat, or even hold his head up as he lay on the floor, stricken by the power of the Living God.**

During other meetings in Western, New York, Finney opened by reading the Scripture in Galatians 6: 7-8: **"Do not be deceived, God is not mocked; for whatever a man sows, that he will also reap. For he who sows to the flesh will of the flesh reap corruption, but he who sows to the Spirit will of the Spirit reap everlasting life."**

It was here that one of the church elders burst into tears, fell to the floor, and began to weep for all could hear. From that moment on, the crowd began to break down and weep in repentance, begging for mercy. This went on for over an hour, having little to do with Finney who had never seen anything like it. It was the Holy Spirit at work, and the work wasn't done until He said so.

During evangelistic services in Antwerp, Finney read Genesis 19:14, where it says:

"Get up, get out of this place for the Lord will destroy this city."

He had only been preaching for a very short time when suddenly he could sense a tangible solemn mood fill the space, clearly affecting the crowd. In a matter of moments people began to fall under the power, crying out to God for mercy. They were all either prostrate or on their knees. Only a few could speak, but all were openly weeping.

ROME/UTICA

I mentioned Rome and Utica earlier in this book. The Rome revival was unlike any other—like a white-hot fire, where conviction fell on everyone within shouting distance. Finney preached every night and thousands came to Christ. Except for a few hours a day, all local businesses remained closed because no one shopped; everyone was swept up in the outpouring of the Spirit. The city had been transformed in a matter of weeks, so that it was scarcely recognizable as the place it had been. In fact, some went from house to house, praying and interceding for each other and sometimes finding people who were already on their knees in deep communion with God.

Pastors from neighboring cities arrived and were astonished at the changes they saw. Conversions were happening at such a rapid rate that they couldn't even get an accurate count. Even people who were passing through town were suddenly convicted and had to pull over to repent. In fact, no one who entered the town could leave unaffected. All were filled with awe, changed simply by being there.

I must reinforce the point once again that because of the powerful prayers of Nash and Clary, the anointing was all over Finney, so that people had only to look at him or be near him to be convicted by the Holy Spirit. I must also add it is not about a man or a personality but one that hides behind the cross that the Lord would be seen and heard. **Living a yielded crucified life followed by fervent intercession brings about great awakening!**

During a visit to a textile factory, Finney saw many people busily working away when a woman met his gaze and then laughed with her friend, clearly annoyed by his presence. As he approached their work area, he felt grieved and suddenly began to weep. When that same woman saw him coming, she grew increasingly agitated and trembled so hard that she could no longer do her work. Looking for a distraction, she strode toward a window and looked outside. He was studying her weaving machine when she turned and saw him then fell to her knees and burst into tears. Holy Spirit conviction caught on like something contagious, until the entire floor of workers were either weeping or had fallen under the power. **In the end, the entire workforce was saved!**

Oh, that the Holy Spirit would once again fall on our workplaces around the world so that entire workforces would be saved! God is raising up glory-carriers in these end times, those so full of the manifest presence of the Lord that it can't help but spill out wherever they are! The Lord is raising up a mature Bride for Jesus Christ. She is prepared and ready to assume her position in His Kingdom.

She is enveloped by the atmosphere of Heaven, and the beauty of the Lord rests upon her. When others see her, they see Jesus. She's been with the Master so long that she begins to radiate the very glory of His presence. **Yes, it's getting darker today. Yes, there still seem to be places that are not open to the movement of the Spirit, but He is raising up a remnant Bride who carries the beauty of the Lord, changing the atmosphere as she walks into every room.** This is our hour and season to be that radiant Bride, to shine forth the goodness of God and see entire workplaces impacted for the Kingdom of God.

Finney himself again admitted that the power lay in the fervent intercession of Nash and Clary. He sincerely believed that his meetings wouldn't have had nearly the success they had without the sacrificial prayers of his support team. Prayer meetings in that day were common and always drew big crowds because people knew that nothing changes apart from prayer. They prayed in public, in crowds, and in secret, convinced that God was a man of His word and would always answer the prayers of the saints, especially if they gathered in groups. They believed that without prayer they were weak, while fervent prayer changed everything. Dare we still believe such things today? What would happen if we did? I daresay that our world would be transformed overnight!

"In regard to my own experience, I will say that unless I had the spirit of prayer, I could do nothing. If even for a day or an hour I lost the spirit of grace and supplication, I found myself unable to preach with power and efficiency, or to win souls by personal conversation. In this respect my experience was what it has always been."

— Charles Finney on Daniel Nash, his chief intercessor.

Chapter 9

THE PASSING OF DANIEL NASH

> **"Blessed man! He was the reproach of the ungodly, and of carnal, unbelieving professors; but he was the favorite of Heaven, and a prevailing prince of prayer."** — *Charles Finney on Daniel Nash, his chief intercessor.*

In his journal, Finney recounted the following details of the Heavenly return to home of Daniel Nash. It was during the frigid winter, on December 20, 1831, in upstate Vernon, New York, when Nash exclaimed that he was dying, when all he wanted to do was pray. He knelt and opened a map of the world and began to travail over the lost in every nation, until he finally breathed his last and went home to be with the Lord. He entered his reward on his knees at the age of 56 and was buried in the graveyard of his previous pastorate with only a small stone to mark the spot.

Perhaps the Lord will raise up others who will stand in the gap for the lost souls of our day, but what would happen if He called you to fill that position? Would you willingly lay down your own agenda to pick up the burden of the Holy Spirit? The marvelous truth is that God is the same yesterday, today, and forever, which also means He could do as much or more than He did in the days of Finney and Nash, but it would take a willing vessel. Does that describe you? **What would happen if the church stepped up to the plate and gave God a chance to do it again?**

These days, there are increasing signs that the church is once more awakening to the truth that it's time to do it again. God is once again laying it on the hearts of intercessors, ministers, and churches to pray far more than they ever have before. This time, there's little pomp and circumstance in the process, only a response to the tender wooing of the Holy Spirit. Both day and night, ministers and lay people are crying out to God, which is paving the way for a widespread revival such as has never been seen before in recorded history. Recently I spoke at a city-wide pastors' prayer event on the life of Daniel Nash in **Fulton, New York.** Dear pastors gathered together for worship and a short word than joined hearts together in fervent prayer. Oh, how refreshing it was to experience passionate prayer going forth again in New York state! Could this be the start of something?

The upcoming outpouring will be much different than those in the past, simply because of the ease of communication in our day and age. Whatever fire is kindled in any location, it will soon spread to the uttermost parts of the planet. The only thing needed to see it happen is **fervent prayers of intercession.** This prayer movement need not begin with the whole church but only a few men and women responding to the wooing of the Spirit, who will not be dissuaded, no matter what. If only these few simply believe His promises, speak them into being, as if they already were, that's enough to bring Heaven to Earth, moving on the hearts of the lost.

May God use this book to inspire many to pray in the revival to come because time is short and Jesus is returning soon!

Chapter 10

RECREATING THE STOW SQUARE MONUMENT

For over 113 years, Stow Square's monument stood proud until a purchaser destroyed the historical edifice because of superstition. As I studied this historical record, I believe the purchaser meant well and was following what they felt led to do; however, these events did cause quite the stirring in the region. Fast forward to 2015; they have erected a new monument in its stead through the passions and donations of the people of Lewis County.

The Presbyterian Church built the original monument in 1899 at the former Stow Square Church. At the time, the area was thought to be the center of the community, but it is really a few miles north of Utica. Silas Stowe deeded the site to the local church in 1803. In 1833, the church formally elected to become Presbyterian and constructed the church building under the supervision of Pastor, Daniel Nash. In the 1840s, the church divided into two congregations and stopped holding worship services in the area. The church was later demolished in 1864.

The community erected the monument in dedication to the memory of the church and a mighty man of God, Daniel Nash. As I mentioned earlier Father Nash was the pastor of the church and renowned throughout the area for his revival meetings with Charles Finney throughout Northern New York as part of "The Second Great Awakening."

The original monument cost only $60. The project was conducted alongside the erection of a headstone at the gravesite of Daniel Nash, buried just north of the original monument. In 2012, the Grace Chapel church that had purchased the land surrounding the monument demolished the historical edifice because it reminded them of "ancient Egyptian cult objects." They moved the base of the monument several yards in front of the original site and erected a cross in the original area. I personally felt the cross when I saw it was far more powerful as a prophetic and spiritual statement than the rock formation was, as it displayed Daniel Nash on his knees in humble fervent prayer. I was moved beyond words as I stood there that day pondering how Daniel Nash was a true humble man of God who literally lived on his knees.

However, this single act of destruction because the monument sat on their legal property caused the memory of the former church and thriving community to vanish. The historical community had once comprised only a farm machinery dealership, a cattle auction barn, and farmland. The Stow Square Monument had initially served not only as a link to the Second Awakening but a message of peace, reconciliation, and love of the Christian faith. The monument was also a favorite destination for school trips where kids learned and embraced the history of Stowe Square.

Many residents were distraught about the destruction of the only standing historical landmark and came together to fund its recreation. In 2014, Edgar S. K. "Ned" Merrell and Lewis County Historical Society got an easement from adjacent landowners

Steven and Marcia Nortz to locate a new monument on the southwest corner of their property at Route 26. Cozzi and Co., a Watertown monument company that also helped build the new monument by erecting the structure at a reduced cost of $8,600.

Several notable organizations helped raise these fees. The Robert G and Florence E Van Duyn Charitable Foundation donated over $5,322 to the project. The Community Foundation of Northern New York, through a 2014 grant from the George Davis Fund, donated over $500. The remaining $1,450 came from the community and members of the First Presbyterian Church.

After three and half years of fundraising, a new eight-foot-tall granite monument was erected several yards away from the original site at the Stowe Square settlement. Though the new monument is not in the old site, it stands majestic and strong as a powerful reminder to the people who will never forget their long history in religious faith.

Chapter 11

A FORERUNNING FERVENT ARMY LIKE NASH, HYDE, AND HOWELL!

"Nothing tends more to cement the hearts of Christians than praying together. Never do they love one another so well as when they witness the outpouring of each other's hearts in prayer." – **Charles Finney**

I n the article "DANIEL NASH: PREVAILING PRINCE OF PRAYER" by J. Paul Reno it states:

"Though he prayed in private, yet he often prayed with such fervency that others became aware of his praying. This was not intended, but simply was the release of a deeply burdened soul. The lady at the boarding house became aware of his groans as he prayed. His enemies claimed, 'that it was impossible for him to pray in secret since, whether he went into his closet or the woods, he prayed with such vehemence that he could be heard half a mile away.' While this was likely an exaggeration of his normal practice, there is a record of a single occurrence of note:

"In the revival at Gouverneur (in which the great majority of the inhabitants, Finney believed, were converted), Nash rose very early and went into a forest to pray. 'It was one of those clear mornings,' said Finney, 'on which it is possible to hear sounds at a great distance.' Nearly a mile away lived an unsaved man who suddenly heard Nash's voice raised in prayer, and no matter how hard he tried he couldn't shake the reality of his urgent need for a Savior. In fact, he experienced no relief until he found it in Christ."

I can see in my heart this man of the country being arrested by the Holy Spirit because of fervent prayer echoing through the forest. I see his eyes well up in tears as he bows his head and humble knees to the King of Kings and the Lord of Lords. May this powerful testimony penetrate your spirit and ignite in you the spirit of prayer!

Lord, YOU are no respecter of persons... What you have done in the heart of Father Nash you can do in me! Give me a heart to pray for revival! Let me invest time birthing the next great awakening while there's still time!

What is fervent prayer? It means being on fire for the Lord and having fire in your belly. It does NOT mean a rambling of half-hearted platitudes recited before dinner or a daily recitation of the ills of daily living. The truth is that kind of emotion cannot be faked or manufactured. It's real and stunning in its intensity. THAT'S what it means to be on fire for God. It comes from love for God and deep compassion for the lost—a true, deep love that's all encompassing and that can't be manufactured either.

There are men throughout history like Father Nash who have lived out that kind of all-consuming passion for the Lord and for their neighbors, brothers, and sisters; men and women who, simply because of their intense love for the Lord, became amazing examples of the power of fervent prayer. In closing, let's look briefly at two more such men. Perhaps in the future I will write more books on more prayer warriors...

Praying Hyde: "PRAYER WARRIOR OF COMPASSION"

John Nelson Hyde (November 9, 1865 – February 17, 1912) was an American missionary who preached in the Punjab of India. "Praying Hyde", also called "The Apostle of Prayer", was the sheer definition of "tireless", seemingly going for days on end without sleep. He fasted often; in fact, food was pretty far down on his list of must-haves. Things that we see as critical to our very existence John saw very differently.

You see, John realized that loving the Lord was vital to his very existence and he lived that Truth, carrying such a massive burden for the lost that he pleaded with the Lord to deliver at least one soul per day or he would not eat or sleep. What commitment! He was remarkable in many ways, all due to his deep and abiding passion for the Lord. He was filled with the Holy Spirit, offering living, breathing proof of the miraculous power of the Spirit and fervent prayer.

John never married, and he had no grand gift for public speaking. In fact, he was partially deaf and seemed somewhat less than enthusiastic, so how did this son of an Illinois Presbyterian minister come to be such a powerful force for intercession in a land of millions of unbelievers in India?

The Word

John had difficulty adapting to the complex language of the land, possibly due to his hearing loss, and so he plunged into the study of the Word of God. In that place, he developed a deep, abiding love for the Lord. As a result, he was truly able to grasp the desperate need for fervent, sincere prayer—the kind that moves Heaven and transforms Earth.

He spent countless dark nights face down on the cold, bare floor in prayer, interceding for the lost souls in India, and his prayer on behalf of others bore remarkable fruit. For the first year, at least one soul per day came to Christ and was baptized. Then two a day and finally four souls a day were coming to Christ because of his fervent intercession. The spirit of intercession was so heavy upon him that those around him would feel that same fervent spirit groaning deep inside them as well. If you visited his room during his many revival conferences, you would find his bed perfectly made because rather than sleeping he would spend his nights on the floor groaning in the spirit for the salvation of the lost. Intercession kept him in prayer right up until the moment the meetings began.

"Give me souls, oh God, or I die!" –*John Hyde, 1910, Sialkot Convention*

John moved people with fervent supplications that appeared to be almost violent at times, and others sought his intercession for Calcutta, Bombay, and other Indian cities, so that the number of new believers grew by leaps and bounds. By then his health was failing, so, at the age of 45, he was persuaded to seek medical attention. The doctor's diagnosis was nothing short of stunning. His heart had shifted out of its natural position on the left side of his chest to the right. Some believed he prayed so hard that it actually changed the location of his heart!

It was clear that his time there was ending, so he returned to his home in Carthage, Illinois, where he lived for two more years. His last words before his graduation to Heaven were, **"Shout the victory of Jesus Christ!"** His powerful intercession led to a wave of revival that swept through India like none other!

Rees Howell: "WATCHMEN TO THE WORLD"

"Intercession prayer is the greatest force on Earth!"—Rees Howells, 1935

He preached that the source of revival was the Holy Spirit, and he and his wife prayed ardently for the Holy Spirit to come. The revivals came, washing over congregations like an all-encompassing wave. —Regarding the Prayer Ministry of Rees Howells

Rees Howells (Oct. 10, 1879 – Feb. 13, 1950) was the founder of The Bible College of Wales. He came from humble beginnings in Wales, where he shunned school to go to work cutting coal in the mines to put bread on his family's table. Later, he sailed to America to get the education he'd shunned and to make some money before returning to his homeland in time to witness the 1904–1905 Welsh Revival. It was from there that he gave himself fully to the Holy Spirit and immersed himself in his faith.

By then he'd married and had a son, after which he and his wife were led to the mission fields in Southern Africa. Both Howells preached constantly and prayed deeply and fervently over the residents of Rusitu, Gazaland and within several weeks their prayers began to change things. **He preached that the source of revival was the Holy Spirit, and he and his wife prayed ardently for the Holy Spirit to come. The revivals came, washing over congregations like an all-encompassing wave.** Thousands received Christ through these renowned revivals, just as Rees Howells said they would, as the Lord had shown him in a vision.

Their work spread, and more souls were saved. Over the years the couple traveled over 11,000 miles from

one mission station to another, carrying their revival blessing with them wherever they went. They
were eventually led back home where God showed
them that they were to build the largest Bible college
in Wales, which became known as the Bible College
of Wales (BCW). But that left a lingering question—
how were they to pay for it? They were certainly not
wealthy, but they obeyed the Lord, had complete
and utter faith in Him, and set about the work with
a grand total of 15 cents between them.

The Bible College of Wales was dedicated on Eas-
ter Sunday of 1924, the result of unshakable faith
and fervent prayer, after many spiritual battles and
tests of faith. The BCW grew in scope and reach. On
a chilly December morning, Rees Howells heard the
following message in his spirit: **"Every creature—
every creature."**

This was a commission from God to give the Gospel to every creature, and it became their mission to
intercede on behalf of those who were lost, to serve
others, and to be responsible for making sure that
every creature heard the message of the Gospel.
The staff **"wept before God for hours,"** utterly
broken, seeing the sin in their own hearts that was

revealed by His light. As their prayers grew more **fervent**, they also felt the increasing presence of the Holy Spirit among them.

Soon the First World War broke out, killing multitudes of people, and their team of passionate intercessors began to earnestly pray for the lost. Rees Howells went to be with the Lord in 1950, but his tireless work, godly vision and lasting legacy of fervent prayer still serve as shining examples of living in this world for the sole purpose of bringing people to Christ.

A Forerunning Fervent Army like Nash, Hyde, and Howell!

All three of these great men were forerunners of a prayer movement that brought transformation to entire countries and regions. Today these men speak a prophetic message to the church of our day, if our spiritual ears are tuned to hear it.

<u>Nash</u> speaks prophetically of a company of intercessors who know how to wrestle in prayer until the answer comes. He exemplified the kind of fervency in prayer that births and sustains a great awakening. Today, rather than one Daniel Nash, the Holy Spirit is raising up a company of like-minded believers who know how to passionately pray until breakthrough comes and lingers indefinitely, ushering in the last great harvest of souls. They are praying for a next Great Awakening and they will see it!

<u>Hyde</u> speaks prophetically of a company of intercessors who carry compassion for the lost. This company cries out from deep within: "Give me souls or I shall die!" They are not content with only their ticket to Heaven; they cry out for the lost, the broken, and rejected ones. They have the character of Christ and flow with a deep humility. They know what it means to pray sacrificially. They weep for those going to Hell; they are moved to pray and do not just mumble obligatory prayers. They have a fervency and fire that compels them into action.

<u>Howell</u> speaks prophetically of a company of discerning watchmen who stand on a wall on behalf of us all and understand and interpret

the signs of the times, praying clear through until breakthrough occurs. Just as it did for John Hyde, the following verse holds powerful prophetic meaning regarding Howell.

"I have set watchmen upon thy walls, O Jerusalem, which shall never hold their peace day nor night: ye that make mention of the LORD, keep not silence. And give him no rest, till he establish, and till he make Jerusalem a praise in the Earth" (Isaiah 62:6-7).

In the same way, this scripture should be one we seek to emulate, believing in a miraculous Holy Spirit outcome. These men were the ones who stood on the wall and would not rest until major shifts took place on this earth. They were watchmen who stood guard, setting their faces like flint toward the Lord, anticipating the coming of Jesus with 10,000 angels to restore all that was lost and release the Kingdom of God on Earth.

In November of 2017, I stood on the old "American Corner" in Rome, NY. As I mentioned earlier, this was the very place where prayer went forth during the Second Great Awakening led by Charles

Finney. Here is an excerpt from his autobiography: **"I should say a few words about the spirit of prayer that which prevailed in Rome during this time. Indeed, the whole town was full of prayer. Go where you would, you heard the voice of prayer."**

In fact, if you walked down the street then, you would often see Christians meet, join hands and pray. Wherever people met, they always prayed. They carried a burden for lost souls and they knew how to travail in the Spirit to see the lost come to Christ. Things in Rome, New York and the surrounding area were so charged with the presence of God that people who entered the region felt that powerful presence in a beautiful way. Tears fell freely there in His tangible glory. Revival had rained down there because of ongoing fervent prayer.

Standing on the American corner that day, I too was awestruck by the intercession that had come forth years earlier and the legacy it inspired. I fought back raw emotions, desperate to see Rome and the surrounding areas host another great revival of intercession and awakening.

Today the Lord is preparing a company of fore-runners that know how to pray and intercede; they shake Heaven and Earth with continuous deep intercession. You will find them lying on the floor in deep groaning for many hours, weeping for the lost. You will find them birthing with travail the next Great Awakening. For even as the Lord used Jonathan Edwards in the First Great Awakening and Charles Finney in the second, there will be a third that will not only hit America but Canada and continents worldwide. The Lord is moving over the waters, preparing a company of intercessors who will pray it in—not just one person but an army of fervent believers like Nash, Hyde and Howell.

I see a cloud moving; the glory is drawing near; the very manifest presence is building and as we pray, the cloud will draw even nearer. The glory is invading the enemy's camp where the people of God will dance and sing again, rejoicing that Heaven is being released. The throne room is cracked open and the very atmosphere of Heaven is leaking out toward the earth. Open your hearts; open the gates for the entry of the King of Glory. Seek the Lord while He may be found; welcome Him in to rest and abide in you, for as He dwells there, the earth shall be transformed. With a kiss of His presence we, as the Bride, shall come forth in His magnificent glory.

Lord, give your people the desire and endurance to intercede again for the birth of another Great Awakening wherever we are! Make us hungry, desperate for a mighty move of Heaven unlike any we've ever seen, that will usher in the return of our soon-coming King!

For as the waters fill the sea, the earth will be filled with an awareness of the glory of the Lord (Hab. 2:14).

"He (Charles Finney) always preached with the expectation of seeing the Holy Spirit suddenly outpoured. Until this happened little or nothing was accomplished. But the moment the Spirit fell upon the people, Finney had nothing else to do but point them to the Lamb of God. Thus he lived and wrought for years in an atmosphere of revival." - Oswald J. Smith

"A prominent feature of the services was the terrible conviction of sin, and many

were shocked at the scenes. Some were on their knees for a long time, unable to utter a word, being in deep distress and agony of soul due to their sins. Others were prostrated under divine influence, unable to rise for long periods of time. Others wept with deep groaning due to the condition of their souls." - The Welsh Revival

End Word

DID YOU KNOW THERE WERE TWO FATHER NASHES?

Did you know there were two great, godly men by the name of Father Nash? Yes, indeed, and I can prove it as I personally went to both gravesites in two separate cities and interviewed experts who knew. In my research I came across a great deal of wrong information on the Father Daniel Nash that this book is written about and sadly it's easily discovered on the Internet. Unfortunately, some information had been credited to the wrong Father Nash, therefore giving confusing information to the public. To set the record straight, I'm dedicating this last part of my book to this misinformation to bring better clarity. I so desire to honor both of these dear men as I believe they both deserve the clarification highlighted in this chapter. I want to celebrate both of their lives as I find them both very fascinating and memorable.

As I dug deep into church records and history, I found two Father Daniel Nashes. To make this clear, I will refer to them as:

1) The Episcopal Father Nash

2) The Presbyterian Father Nash (Charles Finney's Nash)

I was amazed to discover that even today's friends of each Father Nash had no idea there was another man by the same name. I was even asked if I was sure this was true as some people I spoke to had never heard of the other Nash after over 20 years of their ministry. But I assure you that it's true as I personally visited Cooperstown and Lowville and stood at both gravesites, having discovered documented proof of the lives of both men. I'm now seeking to better clarify which information applies to which Nash, which I believe will bring well-deserved honor to each of these men.

The Episcopal Father Nash

(May 28, 1763 – June 4, 1836)

Ordained on October 11, 1801

Great Barrington, Massachusetts (then called Housatonic) was the birthplace of a remarkably godly man by the name of Rev. Daniel Nash, whose example had a lasting impact like no other in the second half of the sixteenth century. He especially left his mark on the village of Cooperstown, where he was the first rector of Christ Church. There and beyond, in Otsego County, he labored as a missionary and became known far and wide to those he served with his love for mankind and passion for God. His grave is marked by the tallest gravestone in the cemetery, in a spot he chose to be buried in.

I visited his grave, which is located on the property of Christ Church in Cooperstown. (Note that I have included photos of my Cooperstown trip within this book.) That afternoon trip to Cooperstown answered many questions and gave me good reason to respect the second and previously unknown Father Daniel Nash.

I visited on a late Sunday afternoon and found no one at the church. I stopped by the gravesite and prayed a short prayer by divine appointment. To my surprise I ran into staff members of the church, who generously offered to show me around. As we walked from building to building, I was able to see pictures of Rev. Daniel and discover more information that inspired me to celebrate his life and ministry. I want to make a special mention and thank you for the kindness of the church staff members who allowed me to enter the buildings and take pictures of my memorable journey. I'll never forget my time there or the special prayers I prayed on those beautiful grounds.

As if that wasn't enough of a blessing, during my tour I found a booklet about Father Nash on the handrail of a staircase. The staff had never seen it before and asked me if I had left it there. I said I had never seen it before either. As they looked through it, they could hardly contain their excitement and were eager to share it with the priest. It was accurate church history, very rare and precious. We shook our heads in amazement at this little surprise, which was clearly an unusual miracle, and I felt it was a sign I was being led by the Spirit in my research.

A Brief Look at the Life of the Episcopal Father Daniel Nash

At the age of 22, he graduated from Yale University along with fellow graduate Noah Webster. Though he was raised Presbyterian, he eventually aligned himself with the Episcopal Church and studied its doctrine. In his later years he was known for this statement: **"You may bray a Presbyterian as with a pestle and mortar, but you cannot get all of his Presbyterianism out of him." When asked about his own conversion, he would reply, "I was caught young."**

During his missionary journeys with Rev. Daniel Burhan, Nash was filled with a passion for Christ that couldn't be extinguished. It was during that time that he met and married Olive Lusk (Birth unknown–1828) who then traveled with him as he ministered. She is described as a soft-spoken gentle lady, and together they made their home in Exeter. Once he earned his church credentials, he was assigned to two churches, one in Exeter and one in Morris, about 18 miles away (29 km).

With an unquenchable burden for souls, Nash simply couldn't grasp the concept of lukewarm Christianity, which was a problem because his superiors in the church were of the lukewarm sort, who, like the Pharisees of old, sought fame and notoriety and had a religious spirit that had little use for passion. In fact, his direct superior, Rev. Samuel Provost, saw the potential for greatness in him if only he would follow in his footsteps. However, he thought Nash to be fanatical about his calling and had no idea why someone as educated and brilliant as Nash would want to work among illiterates who lived in crude villages and wild woods. After that revelation, Nash became very upset and vowed not to seek ordination to the priesthood until that man had gone elsewhere. So, he chose to wait until 1801 and the advent of Rev. Dr. Benjamin Moore, who was installed as Bishop of New York, to become an Episcopal priest.

Through his tireless efforts and constant travel to challenging places, he was, over time, able to raise up self-sustaining churches in the area, and in 1801, the town of Morris saw Zion Church become a reality. It took eight years, but Father Nash finally established St. Matthew's parish in the town of Unadilla and worked to formally organize Christ Church parish in Cooperstown, where he and Olive lived for seven years.

From that time on, those churches thrived, so he went farther afield to preach and shepherd those in a vast number of other settlements, including Richfield, Springfield, and Cherry Valley, Westford and Milford, Edmeston, Burlington and Hartwick, Fly Creek and Burlington Flats, Laurens, LeRoy (now Schuyler's Lake), Hartwick Hill, Worcester, New Lisbon and Richfield Springs—to say nothing of several other counties —which was an almost superhuman task. It was a job he did with excellence, so that he was eventually called "Rector of the churches in Otsego County."

Going back to the story of Cooperstown's beloved Father Nash, it's clear that his travels involved traversing huge wildernesses. In fact, in 1799, Bishop Philander Chase went to visit Otsego County, where he was profoundly impacted by the fact that Nash lived in a cabin of crudely stacked logs, housing his entire family in a barely-livable single room. At the time, he was getting ready to move once again, to an equally squalid living situation where he had driven nails into the logs to hang their meager wardrobe. The bishop helped the missionary move the family's few belongings, but he did mention that they walked to the new place, carrying a basket of crockery between them, and spoke of God.

During his frequent travels, Father Nash rode on horseback, carrying one of his children before him, while Olive rode behind him on the same horse with another child in front of her. She was an invaluable help to her husband because her musical skills were powerfully used by the Holy Spirit, often transforming the hardest of hearts in the services.

Father Nash was nothing if not punctual when holding services, taking his responsibilities seriously, but there were times things didn't go as planned. Otsego County still had large numbers of wolves roaming the area. Even worse than that, one day the entire congregation dispersed to chase a huge bear that had terrorized the area. In the end, they finished off the bear, which was then the part of a huge spread for dinner that evening. While that event had derailed his sermon, Nash cheerfully agreed that it was their Christian duty to protect people, at any cost, even on a Sunday. In fact, that day Father Nash ate himself sick on bear meat!

James Fennimore Cooper never admitted that any of the characters in his books reflected real people, but his book *The Pioneers* is said to have patterned the Rev. Mr. Grant after the person of Father Nash of Cooperstown. Of course, in his description of the man, he personifies him as a rather weak and dispirited individual, while the real Father Nash was a ruggedly healthy bear of a man who was always neatly dressed.

The Christ Church sacristy now houses the only original portrait of Father Nash. It was given to the church by his granddaughter, Mrs. Anna Marie Holland, of Saginaw, Michigan, and his great-grandson, Harry C. Nash, of Buffalo, in 1910 at the church's centennial celebration. At the celebration, Mrs. Holland told an amusing story about the portrait that occurred during her childhood. Not surprisingly, the portrait hung in her father's house, but she found the way its eyes followed her around the room with what she thought was a judgmental gaze frustrating and annoying, especially when she felt guilty of some wrongdoing. At some point, she found his gaze intolerable, so she climbed onto a chair and tried to blind its eyes with a straight pin. The pin pricks can still be seen to this day. I must also agree with Mrs. Holland as the piercing gaze from the portrait immediately seized my attention!

When Father Nash was 70 years old, he was still noted for being upbeat, joyful, and able to see the good side of the worst situation. Even as an elderly man, he enjoyed jokes and was far more fun to be around than most men far younger than himself.

Among the most outstanding leaders of his time, Father Nash has earned a place of honor in the annals of history. A man of boldness and daring, he was always eager to share the Gospel of Christ, ready for any adventure at a moment's notice. He was also gifted with foresight, laying the foundations for future generations that would stand the test of time. In fact, most of those congregations still active today are those he built.

In the *Old New York Frontier Magazine*, this notable statement was written about Father Nash: "No Otsego pioneer deserves honor more—not the road builder or leveler of forests, not the men who fought against Brant and the Tories. To none of these, in so large a degree, can we apply with such full measure of truth the saying that 'no man lives unto himself, and that his works do follow him."

The Presbyterian Father Nash
(Charles Finney's Nash)
Laborer with Finney. Mighty in Prayer
(Nov. 17, 1775 – Dec. 20, 1831)

One hundred miles away from Otsego County, there was a well-known Presbyterian minister by the very same name, Rev. Daniel Nash. This man officiated in Lewis and Jefferson counties, at the other end of the state. It is this Nash that my book is primarily written about: the Nash who labored with Finney. The dear Episcopal people of Otsego and surrounding counties had affectionately called their Daniel Nash "Father," but to the residents of Lewis and Jefferson counties that name identified another person entirely. I find it intriguing that there is nothing to indicate that they knew of the other's existence.

Each man was deeply honored in his own area but unknown elsewhere. What is even more intriguing is that their paths nearly crossed in 1817 when they were within 45 miles of each other holding services. The two men even traveled the same counties; in 1816, the Otsego Episcopal missionary toured both St. Lawrence and Jefferson counties. When I spoke to those who knew and studied the life of the Episcopal Daniel Nash, they told me that he had visited the Rochester, Utica area and were surprised they were not the same person. I was astounded they did not run into each other or meet at some point. If they did, there is no record. I thought I would also mention that the Christ Church of Cooperstown has books written about their Episcopal Father Nash for historical records.

Wrong Information

Some sources state that Father Nash (Presbyterian) was married only once, but I have found research that suggests this is not true. According to historical records both Daniel Nash's coincidentally married a wife name "Olive" and both women were called Mrs. Olive Nash. Olive was the Presbyterian Father Nash first wife. We do not know what happened to Olive, but I believe she probably died of natural causes leaving Daniel widowed.

His second marriage is much clearer. The **Presbyterian Father Nash**, during his first year of pastoring in a union church named Stow Square Congregational-Presbyterian Church of Lowville, New York, married his second wife in 1817 *(Source Daniel Nash: Prevailing Prince of Prayer by J. Paul Reno.)*

As the true story goes, the Presbyterian Father Nash moved to the township from Onondaga County (the area around greater Syracuse). The first census in the area says he owned a farm there by at least 1825. His first year was exciting as a small revival hit his church and at least 70 came to the faith. One of the first he baptized was Sally Porter (December 18, 1816). He married her by February of 1817. He baptized her before the spring and five of her children and possibly a sixth child years later. I have met Nash experts that have traced The Nash family tree to this current day.

There are no known pictures of the Presbyterian Nash. All the images you see credited to Daniel Nash are **actually the Episcopal Nash**! The common picture you see mistaken for the Presbyterian Daniel Nash online originates from the Christ Church sacristy that houses the only original portrait of the Episcopal Nash. I personally saw the huge canvas picture hanging in the building. I turned on the lamp and saw the great masterpiece firsthand! As I said before, the church has other smaller pictures of him posted in the buildings and grounds as well.

Please note the artwork I had commissioned for this very cover and book is actually the image of the Episcopal Nash. I did this for two reasons. **1. There are no known images of the Presbyterian Father Nash and 2. So many now affiliate him with the Christ Church portrait and I am using that image as a point of reference.**

Other than having the same names and traveling in the same circles, these two men were nothing alike. Both were Massachusetts natives, but while the Otsego Nash had become an Episcopal priest, the Presbyterian Nash was a renowned revivalist. The Otsego missionary hated revivals, preferring to see converts trained up in the church to become mature and stable lovers of Christ, instead of flash-in-the-pan Christians who easily wandered off the narrow way. I have to say this was not the case with the

Charles Finney meetings as his soul retention rate was the best in church history. My guess is that The Episcopal Nash was weary with man-centered revivals that had burned through New York. He probably could relate to the burned over districts that Finney spoke about and desired a genuine move of God instead.

The Episcopal Nash is buried in Christ Churchyard Cooperstown, Otsego County, New York and has the most notable marker in the cemetery, while the Presbyterian Nash is buried in Stowe Square churchyard in Lewis County, a nearby forsaken cemetery with only a modest headstone to mark his plot. I felt so grateful to have visited both gravesites and honored the special lives of both of these men with the powerful legacies they leave us all!

DANIEL NASH - AN OVERVIEW AND BIO

> **"Unless I had the spirit of prayer, I could do nothing."** – *Charles Finney*

The greatest wonders of God in American history happened in the time of Charles Finney. This time was referred to as the "Second Awakening" and many cities and regions felt the supernatural works performed through him for decades. However, many did not know that behind this great man stood a fervent, loyal supporter who interceded for the success of Charles Finney's efforts.

History has no record of whether this unique man of God ever ministered outside Upstate New York.

We also know little of his personal life. Today, his tombstone is in a neglected cemetery along a dusty road behind an animal auction barn. His church has since disbanded, and the meeting house can only be identified by a granite step stone. Its wood was used to house grain at a feed mill just four miles down the road. There are no biographies, books, or documentaries written about him. Descendant have been found by the experts I interviewed. His messages (if any) are lost. On a side note, I have prayed fervently that more information would be discovered.

Daniel Nash was a man of great vision, quiet by nature and extremely humble. He was best known as a mighty man in prayer for he prayed in ways that would make many uncomfortable. He began as a pastor, but the leaders of the church rejected him because they felt he was too old. These single acts caused him great pain but did not stop him from seeking another way to continue worshiping and praying to God. According to some researchers, he was Finney's secret ingredient. Charles Finney retired to the pastoral calling three or four months after the death of Daniel Nash.

In 1807, a place of Christian congregational meetings was deeded by Silas Stowe that would serve as a meeting house. In 1819, that unity shattered when they joined the Presbytery of St. Lawrence and built a church. A group sprung out of these congregations and moved four miles south of the village of Lowville, which at the time was a little more than a farmhouse.

Daniel Nash pastored for a few years, committed to the building of a meeting house and the creation of a Sabbath school. However, as mentioned, the church leaders deemed him "too old" to carry out the work of God and relieved him of the position. Although he left pastoral work on the 10th of November 1822, he often came back to preach, baptize converts, and hold communion for over six years after that. God had higher plans for him. He worked as a private intercessor, highly instrumental to the 500,000 Christian converts from Charles Finney's revivals, which is unlike any other in history.

Charles Finney and Daniel Nash first met at the Evans Mills, New York where they formed a partnership. It was here Charles Finney picked up the mantle and evangelized across America. It was at this meeting that Daniel Nash also began his special prayer ministry. During a special encounter, Finney was so moved by Daniel Nash that he called him a man "full of the power of prayer." We can only explain their partnership and goals in the words of Nash:

"When Mr. Finney and I began our race, we had no thought of going amongst ministers. Our highest ambition was to go where there was neither minister nor reformation and try to look up the lost sheep, for whom no man cared. We began, and the Lord prospered.... But we go into no man's parish unless called.... We have room enough to work and work enough to do."

While the revival swept across America, many criticized, mocked, and even persecuted the movement. These individuals ranged from co-partners to jealous ministers and even individuals who had never even been to a single revival. Nash wrote a series of letters about these persecutions written on the 11th of May, 1826. In one of them he stated:

"The work of God moves forward in power, in some places against dreadful opposition. Mr. Finney and I have both been hanged and burned in effigy. We have frequently been disturbed in our religious meetings. Sometimes the opposers make a noise in the house of God; sometimes they gather around the house and stone it and discharge guns. There is almost as much writing, intrigue, and lying, and reporting of lies, as there would be if we were on the eve of a presidential election. Oh, what a world! How much it hates the truth! How unwilling to be saved! But I think the work will go on."

In this letter he discusses being hung and burned in effigy. Here is an account of the very event:

"Swinging above your heads are two distorted figures suspended on ropes. At the touch of the torch, they leap into flames and the crowd screams in sheer delight. Sound like a scene from a lynching . . . a race riot? Not at all. It is a religious gathering. The charred creatures smoldering in the air

represent the public's expression of opposition to the preaching and praying of America's greatest evangelistic team. Charles Grandison Finney and his partner-in-prayer, Father Nash, have just been burned in effigy. Preachers and pew-warmers alike joined forces against the two men who did more to spearhead revival than any other pair in American history."

Although Nash was a quiet man, people always heard his prayers from afar. Many of his enemies feared his praying methods in the same way they feared the evangelism of Charles Finney. One such tale told by Charles Finney recounts the need and power of prayer:

"In this state of things, Brother Nash and myself (Finney), after consultation, made up our minds that that thing must be overcome by prayer, and that it could not be reached in any other way. We, therefore, retired to a grove and gave ourselves to prayer until we prevailed, and we felt confident that no power which Earth or Hell could interpose,

would be allowed permanently to stop the revival."

PRAYER LIST

Their prayers were not without an organized procedure. Nash would always prepare a "praying list" as is a standard tool used by effective prayer warriors. However, he would go beyond the confines of the list because he wanted to be thorough. Charles Finney described this as follows:

*"**Nash had remarkable power in prayer and was in the habit of making a 'praying list' of persons for whose conversion he daily prayed in secret. . . . The answers to his prayers sometimes seemed almost miraculous, for he did not confine his 'list' to those whom he thought might be reached by the revival, but the most obdurate and unlikely cases were made the subjects of prayer, with results that were truly astounding."***

In other recounts, Finney also said:

"Praying with him and hearing him pray in meetings, I found that his gift of prayer

was wonderful, and his faith almost miraculous."

PRAYER OF FAITH

Nash had fervent conviction in a God who answered our prayers, but he also believed that we have a responsibility for the destiny of souls. He understood that this was the sole reason for living: we are all soldiers of Christ and so he gave himself up to be an instrument to spread God's Word. Nash remained in prayer continually because he firmly believed in its power. Shortly before his death, he wrote a letter about the enemies that despised him for his praying methods. His prayer ministry was completely misunderstood while he was alive. As a result, the Calvinists of his day despised and rejected him. Though the letter did not survive, there are excerpts of it from a book written in criticism of his methods. They may not provide all the information, but there is much inspiration in these great words that we must ponder. Here are some of the excerpts:

"Since you were here I have been thinking of prayer–particularly of praying for the Holy

Ghost and its descent. It seems to me I have always limited God in this request.... I have never felt, till since you left us, that I might rationally ask for the whole influence of the Spirit to come down; not only on individuals, but on a whole people, region, country, and world. On Saturday, I set myself to do this, and the devil was very angry with me yesterday for it. I am now convinced, it is my duty and privilege, and the duty of every other Christian, to pray for as much of the Holy Spirit as came down on the day of Pentecost, and a great deal more. I know not why we may not ask for the entire and utmost influence of the Spirit to come down, and, asking in faith, see the full answer.... I think I never did so freely ask the Holy Ghost for all mankind. My body is in pain, but I am happy in my God.... I have only just begun to understand what Jesus meant when He said, 'All things whatsoever ye shall ask in prayer, believing, ye shall receive.'

"I have felt a little like praying that I might be overwhelmed with the Holy Ghost, die in

operation, and go to Heaven thus; but God knows."

Brother Nash died on his knees, praying earnestly, at age 56. To our knowledge, this letter contains the last recorded words he wrote. I find it very interesting that God used his enemies of the day to preserve his words in the halls of history! All things surely work together for our good if we love God! In a world where people are mostly moved by what they see rather than pay the price of prayer, these great words must sink into our hearts. Think about his first ministry years where, although a rejected pastor, he converted over 200 from a population of over 2,000 people. Ponder on the powerful American Great Awakening and then the Fulton Street Revival of the 1850s and to realize the true value of prayer. Fervent prayer makes all the difference in the world! Amen.

Historical Photo Album

The Presbyterian Father Nash
(Charles Finney's Nash)
Laborer with Finney. Mighty in Prayer
(Nov. 17, 1775 – Dec. 20, 1831)

Rev. Abel B. Clary

June 17, 1796- Jan. 1, 1833

*Figure 1 The tombstone of the Rev. Abel B. Clary
located in Adams, NY*

Figure 2 This is the tombstone of Abel's parents located right next to his tombstone

Figure 3 Both son and parents located next to each other.

Figure 4 This is the artwork by Sue Kopczyk of Brantford, Ontario (Healing Rooms) that so inspired my cover and book. We love you Sue and Charlie!

The Episcopal Father Nash
(May 28, 1763 – June 4, 1836)
Ordained on October 11, 1801

Figure 5 Beautiful artwork of Daniel Nash from Cooperstown, NY

Daniel Nash from Cooperstown, NY

FATHER DANIEL NASH
(1754 – 1809)

Reverend Daniel Nash, founder and first rector of Christ Church, energetically preached throughout the sparsely populated Otsego region. Allegedly, Nash chose his final resting place near the church's entrance. An Egyptian-style obelisk, a popular 19th-century cemetery motif, marks his burial place. Nash is the patron saint of the Episcopal Diocese of Albany.

Figure 6 The Tombstone of Daniel Nash located in Cooperstown, NY

Figure 7 The Cooperstown church built by
Rev. Daniel Nash

Figure 8 Located on a church sign on the property in Cooperstown.

Figure 9 Painting of Rev. Daniel Nash located in his Cooperstown Church

Figure 10 A small picture hanging in the Cooperstown church of the Rev. Daniel Nash

About the Author

Steve Porter, Rochester, New York

www.findrefuge.tv

Steve and his wife Diane founded Refuge Ministries and a presence-driven publishing company, Deeper Life Press. Steve is a regular contributor to many prophetic publications including the Elijah List, Spirit Fuel, and the Identity Network. His writings have been read worldwide by hundreds of thousands of people. He also has been interviewed by the Trinity Broadcasting Network and a few other TV programs. Steve's books, articles, and videos have touched countless lives around the world. The Porters reside near Rochester, NY.

Dear Reader,

If your life was touched while reading *Daniel Nash,* please let us know! We would love to celebrate with you! Please visit our website at www.findrefuge.tv

Consumed by His Presence,

Steve Porter

♥

<u>*More Books by Steve & Diane Porter*</u>

Garden of the Heart- *Healing Letters to Ladies*
(Diane Porter)

Crocodile Meat- *New and Extended Version*
(Steve's Life Story)

Crocodile Meat- *Student Version*

Whispers from the Throne Room- *Reflections on the*
Manifest Presence

Limitless

He Leads Me Beside Still Waters- *50 Love Letters of*
Healing and Restoration from Our Lord

Streams in the Desert- *Healing Letters for the*
Wounded Heart

Invading the Darkness- *Power Evangelism Training 101*

Pearls of His Presence- *Intimate Devotions for the Spiritually Hungry*

The Tongue of the Learned- *How to Flow in the Prophetic Anointing*

Draw Me- *The Deep Cry of the Bride*

The Beauty of the Lord- *Your Keys to Radiating the Glory of God*

Daniel Nash, *Laborer with Finney. Mighty in Prayer*

The Stories of Walter Beuttler- *Volume One*

Hidden Treasure- *Intimate Devotions for the Spiritually Hungry*

+ More

Coming in 2021 by Steve & Diane Porter

Beauty of His Holiness- The Great Holiness Revival Is Coming!

His Hands Extended- Stories of Love at the Nursing Home (Diane Porter)

Christ's Golden Queen- *A Prophetic View of Psalms 45*

(This will be book 2 in The Bride of Christ Series)

America's First Great Awakening

For more info and news see our website

*Bulk orders and international orders are available upon request. Email for details.

www.findrefuge.tv

"Making your book dream come true without robbing you!"

www.deeperlifepress.com

New Books by Deeper Life Press

The Narrow Gate – *32 Insights into*
Understanding His Word
By Fran Heron

Living My Dream – *Story of the Power of Healing*
By Londa Choate

Busyness – *The Greatest Threat to the Church Today*
By Bill Dick

God Is Speaking, Are You Listening?-
Prophetic Words that Inspire and Challenge
By Rev. Trudy Daley

Seeds of Faith – *My Journey*
By Melanie Gleabes

In His Presence – *We Have Everything*
By Dr. Holly L. Noe

Catapulted – *Skillfully Navigating the Process of Your Journey*
By Joe Garcia

The Glory Train – *Glory Revival Is Coming to the Nations!*
By Darren Canning

A Life of Miracles – *My Supernatural Journey*
By Dr. Holly L. Noe

Everyday Miracles – *Sixty-Four Stories of God's Love and Power*
By Sherry Evans

Walter Beuttler – *My Spiritual Journey*
By Walter Buettler

Stepping Stones – *A Pathway into His Presence*
By Ryan Miller

Do you have a book in you? NO ONE beats our prices for the value—NO ONE! See the Deeper Life Press website for proof and more!

www.deeperlifepress.com

P.O. Box 21

Shortsville, NY 14548

www.findrefuge.tv

****